W9-BXA-920

DEC 17 2002

CORNING MUSEUM OF GLASS

FLINTRIDGE FOUNDATION

Awards for Visual Artists

2001/2002

Rick Bartow
Squeak Carnwath
Linda Connor
Fernanda D'Agostino
James Doolin
Gaylen Hansen
Mary Henry
Mildred Howard
Mary Lee Hu
Adrian Saxe
Terry Toedtemeier
Patssi Valdez

IN MEMORY OF

JAMES DOOLIN

(1932–2002)

FLINTRIDGE FOUNDATION

Awards for Visual Artists

2001/2002

EDITED BY

Noriko Gamblin and Karen Jacobson

WITH CONTRIBUTIONS BY

Sheryl Conkelton
Noriko Gamblin

Flintridge Foundation
Pasadena, California

34006

This book is published on the occasion of the third biennial cycle of
the **Flintridge Foundation Awards for Visual Artists**.

Published by the Flintridge Foundation, 1040 Lincoln Avenue,
Suite 100, Pasadena, California 91103.

© 2002 by the Flintridge Foundation. All rights reserved.

The Flintridge Foundation does not retain reproduction rights for the
illustrations appearing in this book. Unless otherwise noted, all works
of art reproduced in this volume are from the collection of the artist.

ISSN: 1530-6682
ISBN: 0-9664721-2-8 (2001/2002 edition)

Design
SoS, Los Angeles

Printed in Germany by Cantz, in an edition of 3,500.

Photo credits
Bill Bachhuber: p. 8; Bliss Photography, courtesy of the Buck Collection:
p. 54 (bottom); Brewer Photography: p. 25; Anthony Cuñha: pp. 44, 46;
Donna Endlich: p. 39; M. Lee Fatherree, Oakland: pp. 12–15; Brian
Foulkes: pp. 20, 21, 22 (bottom), 23; courtesy Froelick Gallery, Portland:
all photos of Rick Bartow's work, pp. 8–11; courtesy of Harry Gamboa
Jr.: p. 55 (*A la Mode*); Lewis Watts: pp. 37, 38; Nancy Hirsh: p. 45;
Mary Lee Hu: p. 43; Rebekah Johnson: pp. 9, 10 (bottom); courtesy of
Koplin Gallery, Los Angeles: all photos of James Doolin's work, pp. 24–27;
William Nettles: p. 53 (courtesy of Daniel Saxon Gallery, West Hollywood);
Richard Nicol: pp. 28, 29, 30, 34 (top), 40, 42 (bottom); Gene Ogami:
pp. 52, 54 (top); Douglas Parker: pp. 26, 27; © Regents, University of
California, Lick Observatory, Plate Archive, p. 18 (top right); Adrian Saxe:
p. 47; Wm. Stetz Design, courtesy of the California African American
Museum: p. 36; YaM Studio: p. 22 (top); Douglas Yaple: p. 42 (top);
William Ziegler: pp. 32, 33, 34 (bottom), 35.

Contents

Foreword

The 2001–2002 Awards for Visual Artists are the realization of an elemental goal of the Flintridge Foundation. Since the foundation awarded its first grants, in 1986, a primary goal of the Visual Arts program has been to recognize and support artists and the process of art making both directly and indirectly by providing artists with more time and resources to work. The impulse to create the awards program grew from the foundation's strong belief in the profound dignity and value of a life dedicated to serious artistic investigation. These awards are an acknowledgment not only of extraordinary talent, creativity, and imagination but also of unflagging courage, optimism, and commitment. For the foundation, its board, and staff, the challenge and the rewards of the program are in identifying and honoring the accomplishments, vigor, and determination of a group of exceptional artists who represent the rich variety of visual expression on the West Coast.

The Flintridge Foundation Awards for Visual Artists program biennially grants $25,000 in unrestricted funds to each of twelve individual visual artists in recognition of at least twenty years of continued artistic exploration and the development of a distinctive artistic voice. Since 1997 the program has awarded $900,000 to visual artists in the three western states.

Now in its third cycle, the program has evolved steadily and carefully as we've modified our selection process and criteria to make the program truer to the foundation's goals and to the expectations of our artist constituents. In previous cycles, for instance, the far greater number of applicants from California made it difficult to represent the artists of the three states equitably. Beginning with the 2001–2002 cycle we have delegated the selection process to two separate panels, one to review applications from Oregon and Washington, and the other to review applications from California. Each panel selects six recipients.

Significantly, the criteria for the 2001–2002 cycle were also changed, reestablishing a seminal value of the program—an emphasis on what we call underrecognition. It is our belief that exceptional art has a deeper and more pervasive influence within the culture than is typically acknowledged and that recognition is not always the most reliable indicator of artistic achievement. The foundation's decision to focus on less-celebrated artists is intended as an inclusive act. We are painfully aware that many well-known artists struggle to afford their next creative leap. We felt, however, that giving support and attention to a broader range of talent and expression would be a way to underline our belief that the personal and cultural value of art making is what is truly underrecognized.

Underrecognition is a slippery concept at best. From whose point of view is an artist underrecognized, and by what criteria? Clearly this is a very subjective label. The program's stated goal regarding recognition is to "identify artists who have sustained a commitment to the highest artistic merit in their work, but do not have current national renown. The foundation's awards are intended to recognize the work of artists who have not received solo exhibitions at major national museums, well-distributed monographs, acclaimed national grants, and other means of increasing exposure and creating renown."

For varied and complex reasons, which we are not attempting to specifically address or redress, many artists who have created exemplary work over a period of twenty years have not garnered recognition beyond their region or outside their discipline. A principal goal of this program is to identify and focus, however briefly, on those artists and their accomplishments. Inevitably some recipients will be more renowned than others. A person who is well known in one region or discipline may be effectively unknown in another. By employing a flexible, multilayered definition of underrecognition, we abandon complete certainty, but in return we get the opportunity to increase awareness of outstanding individual talent and to elevate the profile of a variety of overlooked disciplines.

The board and staff of the Flintridge Foundation are pleased to acknowledge the recipients of the 2001–2002 Visual Artists Awards. Presented in this catalogue are twelve exceptionally gifted and dedicated artists who have been selected by panels of professional peers from 1,059 applicants from California, Oregon, and Washington. Their creative accomplishments represent them, their regions, and their disciplines with authentic vitality, originality, and uncompromising determination. We offer our sincerest congratulations for their years of sustained commitment and achievement.

Alexander Moseley
Chair, Visual Arts Committee of the
Board of Directors
Flintridge Foundation

Panelists' Statements

2001/2002 PANELISTS

California Ellen Fleurov, Philip E. Linhares, Larry Thomas
Oregon and Washington LaMar Harrington, Terri M. Hopkins, Beth Sellars

In 2001 the Flintridge Foundation decided to allocate six of its twelve Awards for Visual Artists to individuals from Oregon and Washington. The three panelists for the Northwest region—LaMar Harrington, Beth Sellars, and I—wholeheartedly support that decision. The work of each of the 305 applicants (split almost equally between the two states) was carefully reviewed and discussed. The panelists identified about forty-five semifinalists and then were faced with the daunting task of choosing only six. In the end our decision was unanimous.

The six artists from Oregon and Washington chosen for the 2001 Flintridge Foundation Awards for Visual Artists are exemplary and meet all of the criteria established by the foundation's board. They have been making work at the highest aesthetic and intellectual level for twenty years or more, and they address a broad range of ideas using the tools of fine art or craft. To date, none has received broad national recognition. Rick Bartow is an artist of Native American descent whose powerful drawings and sculptures reflect his heritage and life on the Oregon coast as well as contemporary art practices. Fernanda D'Agostino's site-specific multimedia installations articulate societal concerns such as the inequitable distribution of resources and individual concerns such as the birth of a child or the death of a parent. Gaylen Hansen is an artist and storyteller whose humorous and environmentally savvy paintings depict the foibles of his alter ego, the Kernal. Painter Mary Henry has spent six decades experimenting with nonobjective abstraction, creating works of extraordinary formal clarity. Mary Lee Hu uses inventive techniques derived from the fiber arts to make exquisite metal jewelry. Terry Toedtemeier's elegant photographs of basalt formations chronicle the geologic history of our region. The Flintridge awards will provide the recipients with more time and resources to further these explorations.

The panelists share the hope of the Flintridge Foundation that the recognition conferred by the Awards for Visual Artists will bring the work of these artists to the attention of more people both within and, more importantly, outside our region. We encourage the foundation to continue its awards program, and specifically to retain the category for artists from the Pacific Northwest. It has been our pleasure to view the work of so many exceptional artists and to serve in this process.

Terri M. Hopkins

As panelists for the third biennial Flintridge Foundation Awards for Visual Artists, my colleagues Ellen Fleurov and Larry Thomas and I were familiar with the foundation's commitment to this program and were honored by the invitation to serve. Our five days of deliberation were intense, informative, sometimes frustrating but always congenial, thanks to the superb preparation of the foundation staff. Day one began with a review of the eligibility requirements and selection criteria. After a thorough discussion we were ready to view the 15,080 slides submitted by the 754 applicants: twenty slides surveying each artist's twenty-plus years of work, arranged chronologically and projected four at a time on a wide screen. Close at hand were résumés and supporting material, all promptly and carefully provided on request.

By the third day we had reached the semifinal stage, having chosen fifty applicants while regretfully eliminating many whose work we admired. We revisited the eligibility requirements; maturity of the work was not a question here, but the criteria regarding recognition stimulated intense discussion: "How," we asked, "can such accomplished artists not be widely recognized?" Most, in fact, had résumés listing numerous solo exhibitions, awards, grants, and publications as well as representation in public and private collections. Such recognition generally promises financial success, but this, we understood, was not a factor; we were to base our judgment on the primary criteria of high artistic merit and maturity of the work.

The last two days were difficult. All the remaining work was of exceptional quality. We reluctantly reduced the number of finalists, consoled by the knowledge that many would be selected for the award by future panels. Finally, in the late hours of the last day, we agreed on the selection of six highly accomplished artists: three painters, two sculptors, and a photographer. For me, as curator of a museum dedicated to the work of California artists, this was a watershed experience, one that will affect my role in the future programming of the institution I represent. I know my fellow panelists were equally enriched by the experience and share my gratitude to the Flintridge Foundation's board of directors and program staff for this opportunity, their gracious treatment, and especially the great care and respect they showed for every artist applicant.

Philip E. Linhares

Rick Bartow

Organized by experience, the simple act of doing for years and years a dance of the hand on wood and across paper. Choreographed by a spirit or energy that enters me through my left side and exits in line and form through my right hand. I don't see the future in my work. I do see the past and present in hundreds and hundreds of images that I have drawn. I am myopic, and like a turtle, I move slowly. I see what was, and it sometimes helps me to understand what is. I create because it is my gift to do so. I have a choice— turn my back and it will move on to another, or I can pay attention to it, do my job, attend to my gift, and see what the next line brings.

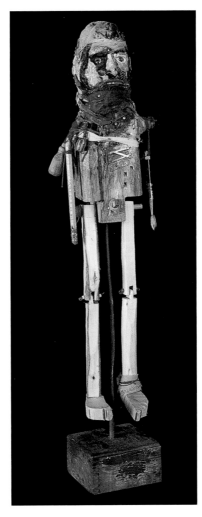

2. **Untitled**, 1995
Mixed-media sculpture; 22 x 4 x 4 in.
Hallie Ford Museum of Art, Willamette
University, Salem, Oregon, gift of Leo K.
Michelson

1. **Big Owl for JBF**, 1998
Pastel and graphite on paper; 40 x 26 in.
Private collection

3. **Stag Man**, 1986
Charcoal, graphite, and pastel on paper; 30 x 24 in.
Private collection

4. **Myth/Reality**, 1992
Graphite and pastel on paper; 26 x 40 in.

Rick Bartow

SHERYL CONKELTON

Rick Bartow's richly colored, expressionistically drawn

figures inhabit ambiguous bodies and spaces, evoking fetishes or shape-shifting spirits. Peopled with archetypal characters, his images are drawn in quick strokes that seem to generate moving edges and telegraph a persistent energy.

Bartow grew up in rural Oregon, near the reservation of his father's nation, the Yurok. In 1969, following his graduation from Western Oregon State College with a degree in art education, he was sent to Vietnam for active duty. He returned home traumatized and spent years trying to numb himself to the horrific memories, falling into alcoholic despair. In 1979 he began to make drawings in an effort to heal his ravaged psyche. Although largely self-taught, he derived inspiration from the work of Marc Chagall, Jim Dine, and Fritz Scholder. His early works—rendered forcefully in dense, inky graphite on white paper—reveal, in their unmediated intensity, the cathartic nature of his art making. Many of these drawings represent animals in the guise of a mask or as a head conjoined to a human body (see fig. 5). "Masks of my own were falling away," he has explained. "I began to be aware of the manifold aspects of our personalities and the way we change."[1]

The transformational imagery that has characterized his entire oeuvre embodies Bartow's own self-regeneration—initially as a human being and then gradually as an artist—as well as his belief in change as a means of overcoming pain. This tenet is expressed in his art through images of metamorphosing animal and human forms, which are rooted in Yurok myths and ceremonies that emphasize renewal and transformation. The artist notes: "There are always animals who are given voices like people. So in a sense, you see animals as being people and people as being animals."[2] The animals themselves—coyotes, deer, crows, hawks, dogs, and salmon—are more than symbols for Bartow; they are his neighbors on the ancestral land that his grandfather settled in 1928 and upon which Bartow still lives.

Several years after he began to draw, Bartow introduced color into his work, at first retaining large areas of the white sheet as an integral part of his compositions. He created a series of shamanic beings (see fig. 3), often combined with the image of his own hand, which became a consistent

5. **Bird/Mask/Man**, 1982
Graphite on paper;
22 x 18 in.

motif in his work. As his work progressed, the color became more solid, the pastel was applied more heavily and with greater gesturality, and a sense of materiality developed. During the later 1980s his growing stylistic facility and fluidity were attended by an increased complexity in the content of his works, many of which describe intricate relationships among figures. His titles often hint at specific myths or other narrative sources, yet the meaning of his works remains elusive and open-ended, a kind of metaphorical reiteration of the mystery of human feeling (see fig. 4).

Since the mid-1980s Bartow has also made masks and small talismanic sculptures, generally of human figures or animals, constructed from found objects, natural materials, and bits of wood that he carves. Some of the figures (see fig. 2) incorporate tools and brushes, suggesting self-portraits—meditations, perhaps, on the artist as self-created being. With their quirky, rough-hewn, and cobbled-together forms, the sculptures are an expression of Bartow's fascination with folk craft traditions worldwide. He has been able to develop this interest more fully in the past decade, for with the maturation of his art in the early 1990s came opportunities for travel abroad in conjunction with exhibitions. Out of a 1997 visit to Japan came a series of works that depicted simple folk figures, Zen Buddhist subjects, and various traditional animal characters. An ongoing influence on his work is the sculpture of Maori wood-carver John Bevan Ford, to whom he dedicated a masterwork of 1998 (fig. 1).

Each of Bartow's works is the record of an intuited vision and a creative journey. Some reference the artist himself; others engage the elemental and humanistic themes of ceremony, magic, sexuality, death, and rebirth. Derived from a continual engagement with the physical and the numinous worlds and their interaction, his art manifests subjective human experience in a visceral conjuring of the psychic and spiritual sublime.

1. Timothy White, "Out of the Darkness: The Transformational Art of R. E. Bartow," *Shaman's Drum: A Journal of Experiential Shamanism*, no. 13 (summer 1998): 20.
2. David P. Becker, "The Visionary Art of Rick Bartow: Works, 1986–1992," in *Rick Bartow: Wings and Sweat* (Portland: Jamison Thomas Gallery, 1992), 6.

1. **Be Happy**, 2001
Oil and alkyd on canvas; 70 x 70 in.
Private collection, San Francisco

Squeak Carnwath

The visible is how we orient ourselves. It remains our
principal source of information about the world. Painting reminds
us of what is absent, what we don't see anymore. . . .
It is evidence, evidence of thought.

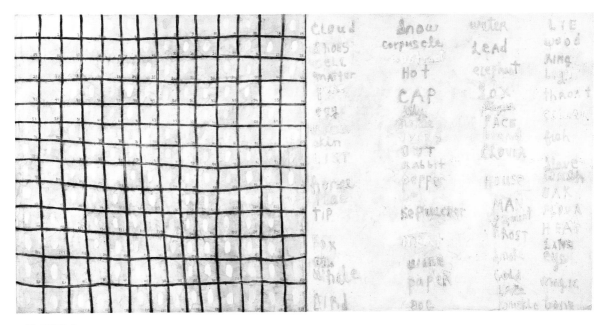

2. **What White Is**, 1994
Oil and alkyd on canvas; two panels, 80 x 160 in. overall
Oakland Museum of California, gift of the Art Guild and friends and family in memory of Anne Gray Walrod

3. **Homework**, 1989
Oil and alkyd on canvas; two panels, 77 x 154 in. overall
Collection of Roselyne C. Swig, San Francisco

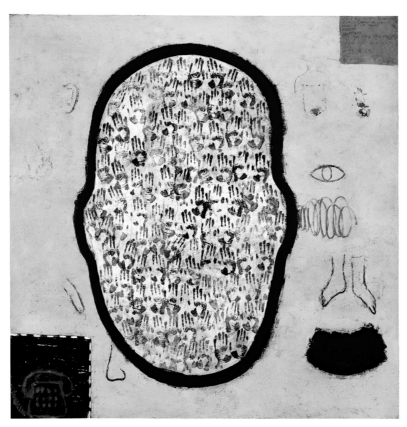

4. **A Call to Be**, 1992
Oil and alkyd on canvas; 82 x 82 in.

Squeak Carnwath

NORIKO GAMBLIN

Born in Abington, Pennsylvania, in 1947, Squeak Carnwath

spent her childhood and adolescence in various towns and cities along the eastern seaboard. After high school she studied art in Illinois, Greece, and Vermont before moving to Oakland in 1970 to attend the California College of Arts and Crafts. Over the next seven years she studied ceramics, painting, and sculpture with Viola Frey, Art Nelson, Jay DeFeo, and Dennis Leon. Soon after her graduation in 1977 with a master of fine arts degree, Carnwath began to garner recognition for her work, including, in 1980, a Visual Artists Fellowship grant from the National Endowment for the Arts and a Society for the Encouragement of Contemporary Arts award from the San Francisco Museum of Modern Art, which included a solo exhibition at the museum.

5. **Day Song**, 1988
Oil and alkyd on canvas; 82 x 82 in.
Collection of Charlie Mitchell, Santa Barbara, California

The work for which Carnwath first became widely known in the mid- and late 1980s is characterized by simple, iconic images and words floating like astral bodies within monochromatic or bichromatic fields (see fig. 5). The images represent common things—chairs, vessels, bones, feet, genitalia, flowers, birds, houses, and so on—using rudimentary forms and emphatic black outlines. The words or passages of text, rendered in an ingenuous and expressive script, catalogue and comment on various aspects of existence, such as the affinities that unite seemingly unrelated objects (e.g., "things that are round," in *Planets*, 1988) and the essential differences (e.g., between "breath" and "death" in *Threshold*, 1989) that divide them. Simultaneously comic and grave in tenor, these pictures evoke the free-ranging ruminations of a daydreaming mind as it encounters the myriad phenomena of daily life and tries to make sense of them. They ask us to consider matters ranging from the mundane ("reasons to wake up in the morning," in *Reasons*, 1991) to the esoteric (the nature of gravity, in *Gravity*, 1988), engaging an ever-evolving constellation of preoccupations and investigations: how we know things, what we know, the nature of memory, perception, passion, time, and death.

Although Carnwath quickly established a distinctive personal style, some aspects of her work have undergone gradual transformations. The strongly geometric structure—characterized by grids, quadrants, and contrasting color bands and fields—of her paintings of the 1980s and early 1990s has loosened into more fluid arrangements of diverse elements, which include structural motifs as well as "decorative" patterns. Similarly, her iconography, which was initially tied to a relatively circumscribed personal symbology, has both expanded and grown more allusive. The early lists, litanies, injunctions, and poetic observations have been joined by more casual notations, which often lend a topical immediacy to her work.

In Carnwath's art, the concept of a consuming philosophical enterprise is not only articulated by pictorial (and linguistic) elements but also expressed in the physicality of the paint itself. Using a variety of tools—including brushes, knives, paper towels, and her (gloved) hands—she creates a wide range of painterly effects through drips, washes, accretions, incisions, and long, fluid strokes—techniques that recall her background as a ceramist. These effects—in combination with a subtle interplay of transparency and opacity that she achieves through the layering of strong, saturated colors—endow her paintings with a highly nuanced material vivacity that is suggestive of living flesh. This impression is critical to Carnwath's concept of a painting as a "stand-in for the body."[1] The articulated surface of the painting represents, in her words, the "whole fabric of reality," with its scarred surfaces signifying "what the body goes through to exist here."[2]

Carnwath's pictorial strategies have, generally speaking, become more varied and complex in parallel progression with her work's thematic explorations. But its content has remained squarely within the broad arena of a personal metaphysical inquiry. Viewed sequentially, the paintings appear as self-sufficient but interrelated "works in progress" within an ongoing program in which life's mysteries, paradoxes, and dichotomies are subjected to an intuitive, sensual process that the artist records through the medium of painting.

1. "Squeak Carnwath," *Works and Conversations*, no. 1 (March 1998): 25; online at <www.conversations.org/98–1–carnwath.htm>.
2. "Squeak Carnwath in Conversation with Richard Whittaker," in *Squeak Carnwath: Life Line* (San Francisco: John Berggruen Gallery, 2001), 9.

1. **Tomb Doorway, Petra, Jordan,** 1995
Gold chloride–toned printing-out paper print; 10 x 8 in.

Linda Connor

I am challenged by using the—presumably—most factual of mediums, photography, to produce images that, though full of facts, are about the unknowable. If there are spiritual properties in art, it seems those powers rest in the attention and focus that art making requires of the artist as well as in the images themselves. In either case, there is little use in trying to explain such things with words. Hopefully you experience it . . . you see it.

2. **Banaras, India**, 1979
Gold chloride–toned printing-out paper print; 8 x 10 in.

765450 RR4123 1/9/03 GIFT FLINTRIDGE $15. EST.

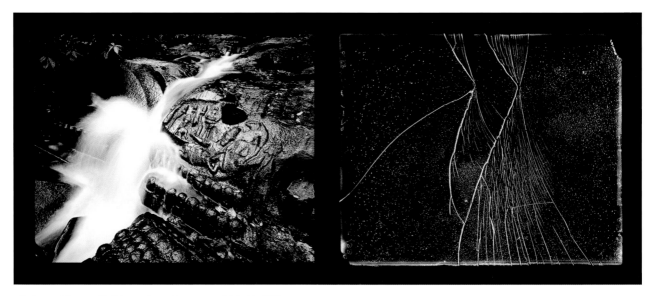

3. **Vishnu and Consort, Kbal Spean, Cambodia**, 2000, and **July 26, 1895**, 2000
Original glass-plate negative for *July 26, 1895* by E. E. Barnard
Gold chloride–toned printing-out paper print; 8 x 10 in. each

4. **Procession, Bali**, 1997
Gold chloride–toned printing-out paper print; 8 x 10 in.

Linda Connor

SHERYL CONKELTON

Linda Connor's images celebrate the complex meanings of

her subjects. Her small, sensuous photographic prints resonate with an abundance of presence, both momentary and momentous. Steeped in the history of photography and its traditions, Connor studied in the famed photography programs run by Harry Callahan at Rhode Island School of Design and by Aaron Siskind at the Institute of Design in Chicago in the late 1960s. That decade was a heady time for photography, a period when all aspects of the medium and its history were considered to be legitimate sources of inspiration, from Alfred Stieglitz to Weegee, Julia Margaret Cameron to Diane Arbus, snapshots to the Zone System. As an undergraduate, Connor was influenced by Walker Evans; she absorbed his willingness to recognize how others create meaning in the world and how the arrangements of inanimate objects around us can speak eloquently about our lives.[1] She learned to look for the essences of things, developing skillful interpretative means to coax elemental resonance and emotional response from her subjects, be they social situations, landscapes, portraits, or still lifes.

5. **Smiling Monk, Ladakh, India**, 1985
Gold chloride–toned printing-out paper print;
8 x 10 in.

Connor's mature work might be dated from 1972, when her methods changed with the gift of an 8-by-10-inch plate camera of Photo-Secessionist vintage that had been in her family since 1906. Its soft-focus portrait lens provided a new catalyst for her photography. The images she made with this camera were the results of new investigations into the nature and quality of light; so too was her concurrent experimentation with the nineteenth-century developing process of exposing the negatives directly onto printing-out paper in sunlight. The subtlety of the paper permits great detail and clarity, and the extensive tonal range, combined with the warm coloration resulting from toning prints with gold chloride, imbues her images with a palpable sense of presence. These explorations culminated in her first monograph, *Solos* (1979), a collection of photographs of common objects that not only displayed her mastery of a process that is integral to her work but also established a signature feature of her oeuvre: a balance between describing reality and suggesting its mysterious, perhaps mystical, import.

In 1979 Connor acquired a new 8-by-10 view camera with a sharp-focus lens and began to travel in the Americas, Europe, the Near East, Africa, and Asia. She found herself drawn to subjects that evoked notions of time and timelessness, seeking out temples, stone circles, petroglyphs, and sacred natural precincts. These travels resemble pilgrimages in that they are purposeful and honoring, although Connor allows that any "enlightenment" lies in the realm of the viewer. Her explorations have resulted in an ongoing series of images that commemorate human aspirations and investigate the symbolic and physical conjunctions between the natural and the sacred (see fig. 1). Among the subjects that fascinate her are paths, roads, and doors—in the words of Rebecca Solnit, "signs that the landscape is already full of eventfulness."[2]

In the mid-1990s Connor gained access to the glass negatives of the Lick Observatory archives of the University of California, Santa Cruz. She made prints from them on site with printing-out papers and paired them with her own photographs (see fig. 3). Some of the negatives (which are more than one hundred years old) evidence the stress of time, and she uses their fractures to evoke a consideration of relative time, human and universal, as well as for their graphic beauty. *On the Music of the Spheres* (1996) was the first publication to present this work, a sequence of photographs that weaves together images of human attempts to create sacred spaces with images of the night sky, its movements and multitude of heavenly bodies. This combination of earthly reality and spiritual desire provokes questions about nature and the nature of belief. Connor's images enlist clarity to invoke wonder, recalling the words of the poet William Blake: "If the doors of perception were cleansed / every thing would appear to man as it is, infinite."[3]

1. Rebecca Solnit, in *Spiral Journey* (Chicago: Museum of Contemporary Photography, Columbia College, 1990), 10.
2. Ibid., 13.
3. William Blake, *The Marriage of Heaven and Hell*, pl. 14.

Fernanda D'Agostino

We are enmeshed in a world layered with narratives, philosophies, and points of view that are rich as well as confusing and contradictory. My work as an installation artist endeavors to bring these unseen worlds to life in a way that allows viewers to move through them and to interact with them in an intimate and physical way.

2. **In Bocca al Lupo (In the Mouth of the Wolf)**, 1986
Collaboration with Dennis Kitsz (sound)
Mixed-media and interactive sound environment; dimensions variable
Collection of the artist, private collection, and Yellowstone Art Museum

1. **Abundance and Scarcity**, 1993
Half-acre cornfield; wood, copper, bronze screen, glass,
and mixed-media meditation house; inscribed copper
stepping stones; dimensions variable
Private collection

3. **Bridge between Cultures**, 1999
Collaboration with Valerie Otani
Structural steel, perforated and laser-cut steel, concrete, brick, glass, metal halogen lights and theatrical gobos, fluorescent lights, fiber optics; 40 x 20 x 200 ft.
Commissioned by King County Public Art Program, Seattle

4. **Fate**, 1994
Video by Kristy Edmunds
Mixed media, wood, aluminum, salt, galvanized sheet metal, wax, concrete, text, video monitors; dimensions variable
Collection of the artist and private collection

Fernanda D'Agostino

SHERYL CONKELTON

Fernanda D'Agostino's installations and public sculptures

engage viewers by evoking personal memories and local histories. In the projects she has created over the last fifteen years, D'Agostino has used architectural forms, handmade and found objects, natural processes, video, and sound to provoke fresh considerations about cultural and spiritual rituals, and about ecologies that have been made obsolete by modernization.

A native of Trenton, New Jersey, D'Agostino studied at the University of Montana, where she obtained her M.F.A. in 1984. While a student, she spent three months in Italy and became fascinated by what she perceived as the relatedness of every aspect of life there—for example, the way in which centuries-old architectural and sculptural monuments coexist with present-day buildings, businesses, and traffic. Resolving to explore this sense of simultaneity, of "deep time," in her work, she created several multimedia installations upon her return, including *In Bocca al Lupo* (1986; fig. 2), in which she evoked a sense of ancient human presence and a sacred precinct. A collaboration with technologist/composer Dennis Kitsz, this work consisted of an environment of forms made of felt and clay (garments, vessels, tools) as well as a musical composition of altered natural sounds that evolved in response to viewer activities.

5. Page from the artist's book **Remembering Our Relative**, from the installation **Imagining the Other Side**, 1996
Cardstock, photographs, and wax; 6½ x 7 x 1½ in.

D'Agostino's investigation of the interrelationships between the individual, culture, and history is often rooted in her personal or familial past. *Fate* (fig. 4), for example, a 1994 collaboration with filmmaker Kristy Edmunds, dealt with life-changing events, taking the Holocaust as a focus. At the heart of this installation was the diary of D'Agostino's husband's grandfather, in which the family's experience of Kristallnacht was described. The diary, veiled in wax, was placed on a stand-up writing desk beside a wax-covered suitcase, an arrangement mutely expressive of fear and flight, and of the human urge to bear witness to life's most terrible moments. While at times D'Agostino draws her iconography from culturally specific emblems (such as a Scottish grave marker or a Latino bridal lasso), her most compelling images often seem to emanate from a personal, unconscious source. In *Imagining the Other Side* (1996; fig. 5), a work inspired by a dream she had following her father's death, seven silver

apples poetically evoke the yearning and waiting experienced in grief, while photographs of family members in the act of recalling the deceased hint at the elusiveness of remembered intimacy. In a more recent installation, *Theater of Memories* (2001), video projections of a bird, a sleeping child, and other archetypal images are juxtaposed with fused-glass wings and cast-bronze rose stems, suggesting both the fragility and the actuality of memory.

A consistent theme of D'Agostino's work is the involvement of the viewer, often as a participant. *Abundance and Scarcity* (fig. 1), which spanned the summer and fall of 1993, was a pivotal work that extended the scope of her multimedia installations into a realm of complex interactions with communities, an element that has characterized her public art commissions of the last decade. Created for Marylhurst College in Oregon, this environmental installation entailed a labor-intensive process performed by the artist and her students, of planting, cultivating, protecting (against predators), and harvesting a quarter-acre cornfield. Both conceptually and literally, the work addressed the uncertainties and inequities of food production and consumption due to both natural and economic forces. It culminated in the harvest of nearly a ton of corn by a local gleaning cooperative, a potluck dinner attended by more than one hundred members of the Portland community, and the distribution of food to needy families.

Since then D'Agostino has produced some one dozen public artworks, often collaborating with engineers, architects, landscape architects, and government agencies on public transportation, park, and hospital projects. Though her permanent public artworks embody multilayered associations, they are refreshingly direct and engaging. The Weller Street pedestrian bridge (1999; fig. 3), for example, executed with her frequent collaborator Valerie Otani, connects an immigrant neighborhood (the Chinatown-International District) to Pioneer Square, the historic center of Seattle. Pedestrians crossing this "Bridge between Cultures" may contemplate, as they view thematic groupings of images laser-cut into steel, the commonalities that link people of different backgrounds, forging the personal to the universal.

James Doolin

*I strive to make my paintings strong on the abstract level,
clear on the descriptive level, and mysterious on the narrative level
so that viewers can make up their own stories and symbols.*

2. **Connections**, 1992
Oil on canvas; 84 x 72 in.
Collection of Ilene and Stanley Gold, Beverly Hills

1. **Psychic**, 1998
Oil on canvas; 54 x 36 in.
San Jose Museum of Art, Museum purchase
with funds from the Council of 100

3. **Corporate Rise**, 1986
Oil on canvas; 90 x 72 in.

4. **Shopping Mall**, 1973–77
Oil on canvas; 90 x 90 in.
On long-term loan to the Oakland
Museum of California

James Doolin

NORIKO GAMBLIN

James Doolin, the quintessential painter of Los Angeles's landscape, came to be so through a circuitous route. Born in 1932 in Hartford, he grew up in Philadelphia and attended the Philadelphia University of the Arts. After serving in the army (1955–57), traveling in Europe, and living in New York City for several years, he moved to Melbourne, Australia, in 1965 with his wife and two young sons. In Melbourne and Sydney he exhibited, to considerable acclaim, his Artificial Landscapes—hard-edged, geometric paintings rendered in bright, unnaturalistic colors inspired by Australia's urban milieu. Despite his success there, Doolin departed in 1967 for Los Angeles, where he enrolled in UCLA's M.F.A. program and pursued his growing interest in a more traditional kind of painting. Graduating in 1971, he embarked on an astonishing project that spanned five years and resulted in a single painting.

5. **4WD**, 1983
Oil on canvas; 72 x 117 in.
Collection of Jay and Ariana Teitzell,
Los Angeles

This work, *Shopping Mall* (1973–77; fig. 4), documents one square block in Santa Monica, the intersection of Arizona Avenue and Third Street. The preparatory process involved obtaining maps, aerial views, and building plans from the city; making hundreds of slides of the area; spending several months sketching and filming on the site; making several full-size studies for the painting; and, finally, chartering a helicopter to fly over the site so that Doolin could confirm his shadow calculations and the color and tonal relationships among various objects. In this canvas, his goal of creating an image with "multiple dramas with every object treated with equal importance and clarity" was magnificently realized in a way both visionary and hyperrealistic.[1] Somewhat reminiscent of the work of the eighteenth-century Venetian view painter Canaletto, and yet thoroughly contemporary in its conception and execution, *Shopping Mall* established Doolin's reputation as a landscape painter of a novel kind. On the strength of this work, he was awarded grants from the John Simon Guggenheim Foundation and the National Endowment for the Arts in 1980, which enabled him to undertake his next project, a series of desertscapes.

These works, executed over a period of three years while Doolin lived in an isolated part of the Mojave Desert, further attest to his unique approach to art making. There is a mystical element to the paintings, which are charged with a sense of the artist's sustained observation of the desert's ancient, alien, but starkly beautiful terrain. Dramatic vantage points and scale relationships contribute to a sense of the series as an ongoing meditation on nature and human existence and on the sheer mystery of inhabiting space in time.

This mystery is particularly apparent in *4WD* (1983; fig. 5), which, with its obtruded view through the car's windows and the menacing presence of a handgun on the seat, conjures up an eerie, emotionally charged narrative. Yet for Doolin the narrative is only a point of entry into the larger drama that the picture presents, which is, in his words, "the organization of color, form, and energy."[2]

Doolin's roots in abstraction are evident in the geometric structure and formal unity of his paintings. Because its narrative aspect is so compelling, however, a viewer can easily overlook the formal mastery of his art. Moreover, since his return to Los Angeles in 1983, he has intensified the thematic (and narrative) content of his paintings to articulate a sublime vision of the city in all of its beauty and ugliness. His statement that "some of the strongest beauty can be found within the 'ugliest' surroundings" elucidates his fascination with the city as a rich source of visual material.[3] He reconciles its duality by bringing to bear various aspects of nineteenth-century American landscape painting—the cool radiance of William Kensett, as in *Connections* (1992; fig. 2); the epic grandeur of Thomas Cole, as in the four Los Angeles MTA murals (1994–96); and the coloristic effects of Thomas Moran, as in *Psychic* (1998; fig. 1)—upon his renderings of a contemporary metropolis. In his large-scale canvases (fig. 3), Doolin presents an awe-inspiring world that defies human habitation while offering inarguable evidence of it, recasting the existential question as a stunned "What (the hell) are we doing here?"

1. Doolin, in Patricia Hickson, "James Doolin's Illusionistic Vision," in *Urban Invasion* (San Jose: San Jose Museum of Art, 2001), 14.
2. Doolin, in James Scarborough, "In Conversation with James Doolin," *Artweek* 23 (3 September 1992): 19.
3. Doolin, in James Auer, "Big-City Squalor Provides a Focal Point for West Coast Artist Doolin," *Milwaukee Journal*, 26 September 1993, sec. E.

1. **Dog and Magpie**, 1990
Oil on canvas; 60 x 72 in.
Private collection

Gaylen Hansen

*I think enchantment, exuberance, humor are wonderful things
to achieve if you can. Knowing all the hazards of life and all
of the tragic things that can happen, I think it's okay to create
a sense of enchantment. If I can do that from time to time,
it's great. That's a form of profundity, I suppose.*

2. **Fish Swimming through Tulips**, 1990
Oil on canvas; 60 x 72 in.
Collection of Linda Hodges, Seattle

3. **August Wolves**, 1999
Oil on canvas; 60 x 84 in.
Collection of Gary Larsen and Toni Carmichael

4. **Interior with Maroon Sofa**, 1987
Oil on canvas; 60 x 84 in.
Northwest Museum of Arts and Culture/Eastern Washington State Historical Society, Spokane

Gaylen Hansen

SHERYL CONKELTON

Born in Garland, Utah, in 1921, Gaylen Hansen has lived in

the palomino hill country of eastern Washington's Palouse since 1957. Its curvaceous landscape and light, and its rural, farming-community inhabitants—fish and fowl, crop dusters and cowboys—are, together with the mythic beings that inhabit his imagination, the subjects of his inventive, exuberant paintings.

Schooled at the University of Southern California in the early 1950s, during the heyday of Abstract Expressionism, Hansen explored and then abandoned that mode of art making, following the trajectory of art into Pop and even Minimalism. He moved away from abstraction in the late 1960s, as narrative content and allegorical representation began to appear in his work. By the mid-1970s he had

5. **Kernal Riding through Dogheads**, 1984
Oil on canvas; 72 x 144 in.
Private collection

developed a distinctly personal, deliberately naive figurative style. His early figures were stiff and hieratic but became increasingly looser and fleshed out over time, both physically and psychologically. He devised a character called "the Kernal," an emblematic western male garbed in a broad-brimmed hat and boots, who is often confronted by freak eruptions of nature, including metamorphosing landforms, giant insects, and strangely knowing beasts (see fig. 5). Dislocating changes in scale and overwhelming colors and patterns threaten to absorb him, and we can see how the Kernal responds to these events, at turns expressing delight, wonder, fear, and equanimity. Ultimately undaunted, he reappears in subsequent paintings to represent human inquisitiveness and resiliency in the face of the unknown and the mysterious.

In the unpredictable world of Hansen's paintings, mundane activities—walking, riding, fishing, or simply sitting—are subverted by absurd narrative twists that recall the western tradition of tall tales. His images thus contribute to a mythos of place, celebrating an indigenous strain of eccentric humor and self-identity. The improbable predicaments that devolve from Hansen's entertaining the question "What if?" feature a fairly consistent cast of native creatures, including magpies, grasshoppers, bison, dogs, ducks, and horses. As opposed to the Kernal, such creatures often represent the natural forces of which this region's inhabitants are

powerfully aware: the fecundity and wildness of life's cycles as observed through wildlife and the seasons. In the large-scale painting *Interior with Maroon Sofa* (1987; fig. 4), for example, the grasshopper's burlesque proportions invest it with a cartoonlike quality that recalls the quirky surrealistic paintings of Bay Area artist William Wiley. In other works, such as *Dog and Magpie* (1990; fig. 1), Hansen's creatures appear as consciously focused presences, as complex—and as enigmatic—as any human ones.

The fantasy and hyperbole that characterize Hansen's narratives have their stylistic counterpart in the colorful, riotous patterning that is a signature element of his work. *Fish Swimming through Tulips* (1990; fig. 2), for example, presents a memorable image of fish coursing through a medium of long-stemmed red tulips. Hansen's interest is clearly not only in the image's inherent strangeness but also in the fluid, allover pattern of interlocking shapes and color that such a juxtaposition occasions. In their compositional clarity and dynamism, paintings such as this remind us of the artist's grounding in American abstraction. In other works Hansen creates visual drama through the relationship of figure to ground—generally, simplified figures against flattened, proscenium-like spaces—which underscores the theatrical aspect of storytelling in his art. He draws on a variety of influences; paintings by the French *primitif* Henri Rousseau, medieval and Mughal miniatures, Egyptian tomb paintings, and Giorgio Morandi's ascetic still lifes are all examples to be mined in the solving of pictorial problems.

Hansen works out his compositions in loose drawings on paper and then on canvas, using strong two-dimensional movements across the picture plane and animating the negative spaces as the imagery gains form. His spontaneous drawings develop into finished tableaux through the application of thick, tactile paint that is brushed, ragged, and bladed onto the canvas. The two-dimensionality of the subjects further foregrounds the paint and painting activity. Hansen's canvases are antic and virtuosic acts of art making; the vitality of their subjects expresses a deep love of and respect for the medium and its possibilities.

1. **Giverny #2**, 1985
Acrylic on canvas; 72 x 96 x 2 in.

Mary Henry

As I matured and became more thoughtful about what I was doing, I began to perceive the geometry of all life, from its infinitesimally small parts to the structure of the universe. I began to try to capture the way I felt about this universe to which I belonged, and to see the images of my mind made real.

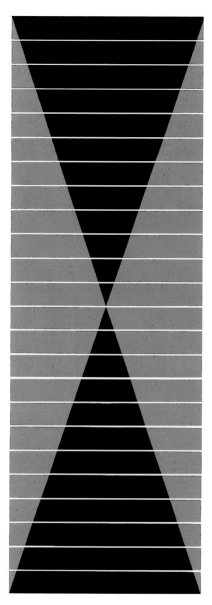

2. **Nexus II**, 1965
Acrylic on canvas; 72 x 49½ x 2 in.

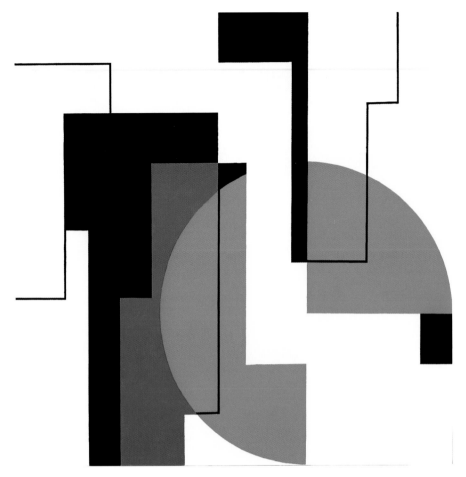

3. **Red Fracture**, 2001
Acrylic on canvas; 54 x 54 x 2 in.

4. **Dark Ascension**, 1974
Acrylic on canvas; 72 x 144 x 2 in.

Mary Henry

NORIKO GAMBLIN

In recent years Mary Henry (who turns eighty-nine this year) has finally received recognition as one of the outstanding abstract painters working in the Pacific Northwest. Born in Sonoma County, California, Henry enrolled in the California College of Arts and Crafts in Oakland, where she studied the fundamentals of painting, drawing, pottery, weaving, metalwork, and jewelry. An array of job assignments and relocations followed her graduation in 1938. In 1945 she enrolled in Chicago's Institute of Design (founded in 1937 as the New Bauhaus), where she studied drawing, photography, architecture, and sculpture. One of her teachers there was the institute's founder, László Moholy-Nagy (1895–1946), whose investigations of the interrelationship of space, time, and light, and whose abstract, geometric vocabulary critically influenced Henry's development as an artist. Familial obligations and financial pressures prevented her, however,

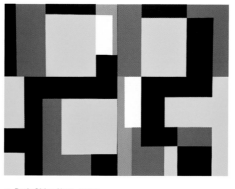

5. **Both Sides Now**, 1989
Acrylic on canvas; 72 x 96 x 2 in.
Private collection

from devoting herself to her art until the mid-1960s. As a divorcee with two grown children operating a bed-and-breakfast in Mendocino, California, she finally had an opportunity to pursue a focused exploration of the artistic concerns that she had identified twenty years earlier.

Henry's work from this period is exemplified by the elegant and masterful *Nexus II* (1965; fig. 2), a large-scale painting composed of triangular fields of green and black flanked by broad white margins and articulated by a narrow horizontal grid. Unequivocal in its frontality, symmetry, and simplicity, the work illuminates a central tenet of her approach: "In my paintings I wanted clarity and order, and so I constructed them as I would a piece of architecture."[1] In its subtle geometric illusionism this painting simultaneously acknowledges the ambient influence of Op Art—an influence that would become overt in the On/Off series of the late 1960s. The illusion of a gentle outward curve at the outer sides of the point where the two green triangles meet is held tensely in check by the white margins of the painting, which seem to exert an inward pressure. This compositional tension, which generally characterizes Henry's work, is especially evident in paintings of the following decade, such as

Dark Ascension (1974; fig. 4), with its austere, architectonic structure, as well as a meditative quality that recalls the canvases of Mark Rothko. Henry's paintings of the 1980s and 1990s evidence her experimentation with compositions that maintain a rigorous clarity of structure while orchestrating more complex interplays of color and shape. Various factors in her life—including travel in Alaska and Europe, as well as her purchase of a home and land on Whidbey Island, Washington—inspired new ways of conceiving the two-dimensional space of the canvas in relation to the three-dimensional world.

Although it bears—and, indeed, invites—speculation, Henry's iconography remains tantalizingly elusive. For Henry, as for her mentor, Moholy-Nagy, geometric forms—circles, squares, rectangles, strips, and triangles—possess no specific meanings per se but, in juxtaposition with one another, express interrelationships among things—both animate and inanimate—that exist in the world. Thus, for example, *Giverny #2* (1985; fig. 1), which was inspired by a visit to the luxuriant garden of French Impressionist painter Claude Monet, describes Henry's experience of its space and light through a dynamic disposition of intersecting shapes and contrasting bands of emphatically nonliteral color. "I am not interested in portraying life as such, but I am interested in portraying ideas and emotions," she has stated.[2] The titles of her paintings offer clues about her responses not only to landscape, both natural and constructed, but also to music, literature, and art itself. In *Both Sides Now* (1989; fig. 5), a rhythmic pattern of squares and rectangles suggests the cascading melody of a popular song of the 1960s, while *Red Fracture* (2001; fig. 3) conveys a dual sense of rupture and balance through a play of geometric forms across the surface of the canvas. For Henry, the beauty and abiding contemporaneity of a modernist geometric language reside in its ability to distill the logic and harmony that underlie all things into images that are both potent and lyric.

1. Artist's statement, 2001 (Flintridge award application).
2. Ibid.

Mildred Howard

*There is a sense of congregation in my work. The congregation is
moving somewhere. A movement toward the potential birth of a
people or the birth of an idea confronts the issues of race, gender,
culture, and religion. These groups are not moving in the real
world but are a presence of memory or an anticipation
of the future, an intuition of what lies ahead.*

2. **Crossings**, 1997
Mixed-media installation: painted walls, ambient light, ceramic eggs, antique gilded mirror; 45 x 54 ft.
Installation at the Berkeley Art Center

1. **Memory Garden: Phase II**, 1990
Mixed-media installation: sand, glass bottles, birch trees,
text (rear wall), ambient light; dimensions variable
Installation at the California African American Museum

3. **Abode: Sanctuary for the Familia(r)**, 1994
Mixed-media installation: painted walls, blue glass bottles, wood, sand, roses (on floor of house); 40 x 60 ft. (variable)
San Jose Museum of Art, promised gift of Katie and Drew Gibson

4. **Tap: Investigation of Memory**, 1989
Mixed-media installation: antique
shoe-shine stand, metal shoe
taps, shoes, ambient sound;
10 x 13½ x 51½ ft. (variable)
San Francisco Art Institute

Mildred Howard

"The youngest of ten children, born in San Francisco,

raised in Berkeley, I have lived all my life within a ten-block radius of my childhood home."[1] Thus begins a recent essay by Mildred Howard, a sculptor and installation artist who has explored issues of personal and cultural identity since the late 1970s. This statement reflects a principle that is at the heart of her life and work. According to Howard, "black people have to remember their families and those who are close to them."[2] Her rootedness constitutes, in a most literal sense, a continual act of remembering her past, but it also bears witness to her belief that the key to understanding the world is buried in the ground beneath one's feet.

For Howard, that ground is unusually fertile. Born to parents who were simultaneously antique restorers and dealers, shipyard workers, union activists, and civic leaders, Howard also belonged to a culturally lively community. By the age of five, she had been introduced to painting and crafts, ballet, and music through programs at a nearby church, with the result that "I became a person who makes things."[3] The things she has made over the course of her artistic career often refer to her family history and her community. But the essential issue in much of her work—the struggle for livelihood, dignity, and equality, and the dire necessity of preserving it in memory—easily encompasses a national and global community.

Howard has employed a wide range of media and approaches. Inspired by Valentine's Day candy, *Some Mo' of Dem Chocolate Hearts* (1979; fig. 5) features assorted "candies," some wrapped in stereotypical images of African Americans, and others in images drawn from old family photographs. Within the arena of a small heart-shaped box, Howard presents the coexistence of crude fictions along with little-known realities of African American life. She developed this simple duality into a more complex aggregate of concerns during the 1980s. A full-scale installation, *Tap: Investigation of Memory* (1989; fig. 4) was intended as an homage to tap dancers and shoe shiners and, more generally, to the lost and forgotten contributions of many Americans. Arranging ordinary shoes (which she had gessoed white) and hundreds of rows of taps (each inscribed with the word *Traveler*)

5. **Some Mo' of Dem Chocolate Hearts**, 1979
Fabric, photographic images;
21 x 21 x 2 in.
Collection of Betye Saar, Los Angeles

before an old-fashioned shoeshine stand, Howard invoked the dignity of a stigmatized occupation. In their uniformity and repetition, the taps create an impression of a consensus of innumerable, unheard voices (or feet), as well as evoking the staccato rhythm of the dance itself.

The repetition of a single common object is a device Howard employs to eloquent effect in many of her installation works, perhaps most notably in *Memory Garden* (1990; fig. 1), a work inspired by the 1912 autobiography of James Weldon Johnson (a statesman and cofounder of the NAACP). In the various incarnations of this work, Howard has used bottles, upended in the sand or forming the walls of remarkable bottle houses (see fig. 3). In her hands the bottle suggests the old South (where half-buried, upside-down bottles frequently lined garden borders); bottles used to keep the "vexes," or bad spirits, away (a tradition from Africa's West Coast); and, relatedly, the bottle trees and houses found in various parts of the world. It is an object with ties to African American tradition, as well as to more universal social rituals involving drinking, conjuring associations of luck, mysticism, desperation, and celebration. Beyond these associations, however, the bottle is also an object made of splendid, luminous material that demands aesthetic contemplation. In this work, for example, which was installed in an atrium, daylight shone through bottles that were etched with words, projecting patterns on the sand and the floor.

For Howard, beauty is a necessary "hook." A teacher herself, she has written of understanding as a slow sinking-in process.[4] With Howard's works, strong—even startling—initial impressions burn into the mind, developing more complex meanings over time. The unforgettable image—composed of ordinary, devalued objects—is tied to an exhortation to remember what it means to be human.

1. Artist's statement, 2001 (Flintridge award application).
2. Howard, in Meredith Tromble, "A Conversation with Mildred Howard," *Artweek* 24 (16 December 1993): 19.
3. Ibid.
4. "This Larger Thing in the World," *Works and Conversations*, no. 3 (March 2000): 36.

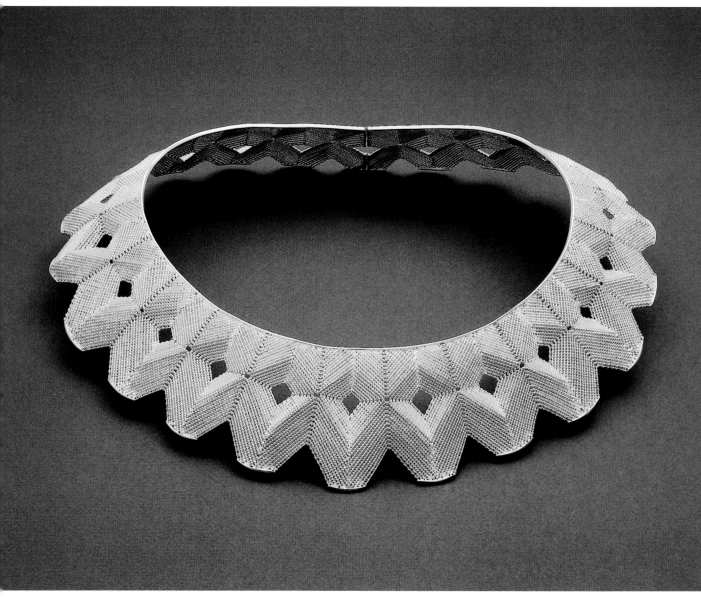

1. **Choker #70**, 1985
Twined and constructed 18- and 22- karat gold; 6 x 9½ x 3 in.
Collection of Donna Schneier, New York

Mary Lee Hu

I am interested in the whole range of jewelry (read body adornment) and other small personal objects, and their connection to people in their cultures. . . . Along with wishing to be able to place historic/ethnographic pieces into a cultural context, I am also interested in how my own pieces, and the field of contemporary jewelry with which I identify, fit into our current society.

2. **Neckpiece #26**, 1976
Coiled and constructed sterling silver and 14-karat gold; 11 x 6¼ x 1 in.
Yale University Art Gallery, New Haven, CT, Bradford F. Swan, B.A. 1929, Fund

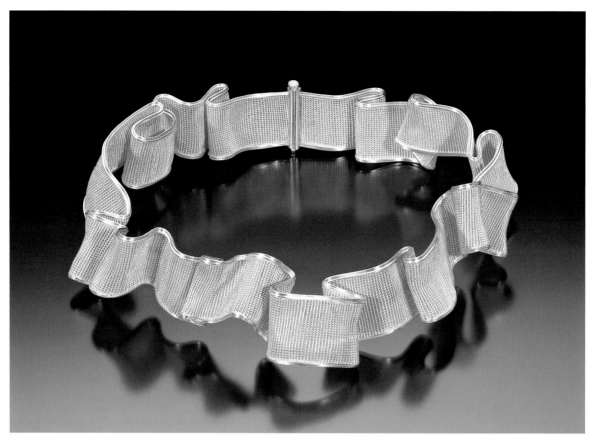

3. **Choker #83**, 2000
Twined and constructed 18- and 22- karat gold; 6¼ x 6½ x 1¾ in.

4. **Choker #78**, 1991
Twined and constructed 18- and 22- karat gold; 6⅜ x 8⅞ x 1½ in.

Mary Lee Hu

The technical demands of working in a medium that has

been categorized as craft, and whose territory ranges widely over artistic and commercial applications, requires a steady, consistent sense of self and purpose. Mary Lee Hu was introduced to metalwork when she took a course in the subject while attending high school. In the decades since, she has evolved into an artist of technical brilliance who has earned international recognition for her jewelry and small sculpture.

Hu studied in the Midwest, earning her undergraduate degree from Cranbrook Academy of Art and a master of fine arts degree from Southern Illinois University at Carbondale. In graduate school during the mid-1960s she continued to work with metal, whose "gentle resistance to being formed," as well as "the reflection of light from its surface," had long captivated her.[1] After taking a fiber arts class, she began to apply traditional textile techniques—including twisting, wrapping, braiding, and knotting—to her metalwork. Her first

5. **Bracelet #17**, 1982
Twined and constructed fine and sterling silver, 14-karat gold; 3½ x 4 x ¾ in.

works were low-tech, their handmade character an important aspect of their content.

Hu was living in Taiwan with her mathematician husband when he died suddenly in 1972. She remained there with his mother for a year, continuing her exploration of wire techniques as she began to incorporate Chinese motifs into her jewelry designs. Before returning to the United States in 1973, she spent three months traveling with her father in Southeast Asia and the Middle East, exploring the cultures of some fifteen countries and studying their metalwork traditions. This understanding formed the foundation of Hu's interest in jewelry as cultural expression, and in the links between certain forms and materials and particular traditions. Since that time she has built up a broad knowledge of historical and contemporary practices, which she mines in the creation of her own works. For example, in *Choker #70* (1985; fig. 1), a work celebrating the soprano Elizabeth Rethberg's feature role in Verdi's *Aida*, Hu conceived the negative spaces articulated by a series of *X*'s as the unifying motif in a commanding neckpiece. She realized her original design in the deep yellow, high-karat gold associated with Egypt, where the opera is set. Similarly, a stunning series of

chokers and bracelets that she produced in the early 1980s (see fig. 5) are adapted from the torque, a metal collar worn by ancient Celts.[2]

Hu's ability to conjure associations with historical traditions has its basis not only in her deployment of a wide-ranging stylistic vocabulary but also in her mastery of the craft of metalwork. A pivotal moment in her technical evolution came in 1974, when she began to twine metal wire. In her own words, she "became intrigued by the architecture or engineering of weaving."[3] Using wire of precious metals (at first fine and sterling silver and then, beginning in 1985, eighteen- and twenty-two-karat gold), she adapted the basketry technique of twining to her chosen material. Hu is much admired for her use of the double-twining technique (in which double strands of gold wire are twined around heavier gold warps) to produce the complex constructions of her signature works. These shapes possess three-dimensionality and weight and are often incorporated into larger configurations that exploit positive and negative spatial relationships in graphic plays of light and shadow.

In keeping with her professed love of "pattern, rhythm and symmetry,"[4] much of Hu's work is animated by line rather than mass. Her early style of the 1970s was characterized by flamboyant, organically derived figurative forms (see fig. 2). Since around 1980, however, her work has tended increasingly toward an abstract geometric structure as dictated—and allowed—by the refinement of her techniques. The range of expression is considerable: some works possess the measured visual rhythm of mosaic tiles, while in others the metal is manipulated to appear almost fluid in a loosening of warp-and-weft rectangularity (see fig. 3). What remains constant within an oeuvre that has spanned three decades is an implicit declaration of the potency of these works, both as compelling physical objects and as multivalent signifiers of personal and cultural identity.

1. Mary Lee Hu, artist's statement, 2001 (Flintridge award application).
2. Susan Biskeborn, *Artists at Work* (Seattle: Alaska Northwest, 1990), 145.
3. Robin Updike, "Weaving Metal," *Fiberarts* 24 (summer 1997): 42.
4. Hu, artist's statement, 2001.

Adrian Saxe

*My ceramic work explores the possibilities of a meaningful
and significant traditional art, open to all of its manifestations
and implications in a rapidly changing postmodern global
cultural arena. I make work that aggressively projects my
sensibilities and formal interests while extending and
critiquing the intellectual and formal traditions of art.
I am the "village potter"—for the global village.*

2. **Untitled Ewer (Aubergine)**, 1982
Porcelain, gold lusters; 10 x 8 x 3 in.
Collection of George and Dorothy Saxe, Palo Alto, Calif.

1. **Untitled Théière (PAA)**, 2000
Porcelain, stoneware, rhinestones;
13 ⅜ x 8 ⅝ x 4 ⅛ in.
Collection of Jerry and Lynn Howe Myers,
South Pasadena, Calif.

3. **Untitled Gold Bowl (Big Red)**, 1987
Porcelainous stoneware with raku
base; 17 x 19½ x 12 in.
Collection of Mr. and Mrs. Larry
Zellner, Franklin Lakes, N.J.

4. **Untitled Ewer (St. Vincent)**, 1995
Porcelain and stoneware;
16¼ x 11½ x 5¼ in.
Collection of Jerry and Lynn Howe
Myers, South Pasadena, Calif.

Adrian Saxe

NORIKO GAMBLIN

Over the past three decades Adrian Saxe, one of the

foremost artists working in ceramics in the United States, has created a body of work so unique that it is often considered to be in a category of its own. His training was not unusual; he studied art at the University of Hawaii in the early 1960s and attended Chouinard Art School in Los Angeles from 1965 to 1969. But his interests in the medium ran counter to dominant trends in American ceramics of the 1950s and 1960s, which merged aspects of Japanese folk pottery with the robust physicality associated with Abstract Expressionist painting. Saxe, by contrast, was fascinated by traditional European and Chinese vessels (constructed through additive methods) and lacquerwork and, simultaneously, by Los Angeles's contemporary "finish fetish" movement, characterized by seamless, high-gloss surfaces that recall those of cars and surfboards.

In 1969, when financial difficulties forced him to leave school, Saxe supported himself by producing porcelain mugs as well as pottery that explored various historical genres and materials. The following year, he received a commission to make a group of jardinieres for the Henry E. Huntington Library and Art Gallery in San Marino, California, whose ceramic collections, both Asian and

5. **Untitled Covered Jar with Antelope Finial**, 1973
Porcelain and stoneware;
19¾ x 6½ in.
Collection of Ken Deavers,
Washington, D.C.

European, had been a source of inspiration since he first saw them as a teenager. The commission provided him with an opportunity to pursue his particular interest in Baroque and Rococo European ceramics, which included genres that were categorically dismissed by his contemporaries as moribund and irrelevant. The result of this engagement was a more fully articulated direction in his studio practice, toward more complex vessels that incorporated his reinterpretations of diverse ceramic traditions.

In 1973 Saxe began teaching full-time at UCLA, where he is now the head of the ceramics program. Having been captivated by animal motifs (such as rams and stags) found on European ceramics and silver, he began to produce vessels with lids topped by antelopes and other animal figures. Rendering the animals prominently, and in all their majestic angularity, he played off the incongruity between

the elegant, unwieldy "lifting devices" and the utilitarian conceit of the jar form. These "antelope jars" of the 1970s and early 1980s (see fig. 5) form the basis of Saxe's ongoing exploration of functionality in ceramics as an expression of aesthetic ritual—one with conceptual, rather than literal, ties to utilitarian concerns. It was in this body of work that he also determined a personal approach to constructing meaning through sets of formal and thematic oppositions: natural versus cultural, geometric versus organic, static versus dynamic, traditional versus contemporary, East versus West, refined versus crude, high versus low, serious versus fanciful, precious versus cheap. These dualities appear as witty, often burlesque juxtapositions of contrasting elements, as exemplified by a ewer in the form of an eggplant with elaborate gold fittings (fig. 2). Yet they are integrated into works of remarkable presence, which, in their dialectical play, provoke reflection upon a broad range of cultural issues.

The sense of surprise and wonderment that precedes—and occasions—such reflection is due in large measure to the immense technical virtuosity evident in all of Saxe's work. It is a mastery that he has developed throughout his career but that he pursued with particular rigor during the 1970s and 1980s, when he experimented with molds, glazes, and various firing techniques. His research took him to France in 1983 on a six-month fellowship to work as a visiting artist at the Manufacture nationale de Sèvres, whose technical attainments he had long admired. The residency resulted in his expansion and clarification of issues that lie at the core of his practice, including ceremonial function, luxury, presentation, and display. The work he has produced since that time reveals a staggering variety of new and hybrid forms—more organic and complex (see fig. 4), often featuring bases in dramatically contrastive styles and textures (see fig. 3). Rich in meaning and material, Saxe's creations continue to push his medium in new directions—formally, technically, and conceptually—challenging the viewer to think in new ways about the ceramic arts.

47

Terry Toedtemeier

As the nature of human life and our knowledge of ourselves and our universe gain bewildering levels of complexity, the quest for unity becomes increasingly important. Without it, things have no meaning, no place in a "larger scheme of things." The pervasive existence of beauty is a quality that I value greatly. I've become attracted to depicting specific geologies as a way to express beauty inherent in the world through time.

2. **Entrance to Sea Cave, Cape Lookout State Park, Oregon**, 1998
Selenium-toned gelatin silver print; 14 x 18 in.

1. **Archway in Basalt Headland, Lincoln County, Oregon**, 1992
Selenium-toned gelatin silver print; 18 x 9 in.

3. **Sub-Zero Fog, Crack in the Ground, Lake County, Oregon**, 1993
Selenium-toned gelatin silver print; 11 x 22 in.

4. **Arch in Pillow Basalt, Multnomah County, Oregon**, 1987
Selenium-toned gelatin silver print; 9 x 12 in.

Terry Toedtemeier

SHERYL CONKELTON

Geology, the subject that Terry Toedtemeier studied in

college, is now the subject studied in his photographs— meditative images of sublime beauty that require a slowed-down contemplation. He portrays the history of weathered landforms, conjuring tectonic movements, vast eruptions, and the slow reshaping of the earth, so that each photograph becomes a particular moment that speaks of eons of activity on a scale that dwarfs the human.

As a photographer of the western landscape, Toedtemeier is heir to a grand and influential tradition that includes Carleton Watkins and Ansel Adams, photographers whose visions of a paradisiacal wilderness were instrumental in shaping an American national identity. Toedtemeier, who has been curator of photography at the Portland Art Museum since 1983, is intimate with this history. Certain aspects of his work reveal his affinity for this landscape tradition, particularly Watkins's characteristic compositional balance, which suggests the equilibrium of forces contained within earthly masses. But, overall, as writer Christopher Zinn has observed, Toedtemeier displays a "sensitivity to landscape forms that are, in the first instance, less picturesque than the vistas typically associated with our region. It's as if he wants to extricate his own eye from the commandeering visual habits of the landscape tradition."[1]

The formation of Toedtemeier's vision of landscape has, in fact, less to do with an artistic tradition than with his native proclivities. As a child he was a rock hound; later he studied geology at Oregon State University. While a student, he spent a summer mapping geologic formations in eastern Oregon—a revelatory experience that he summed up as follows: "Visible geological form had become both symbol and evidence of the inner workings of the earth."[2] Following his graduation in 1969, Toedtemeier began to experiment with photography as an artistic rather than a documentary medium. His early photographs were close-range images of human gestures and interactions (for example, a woman brushing her hair), some of them humorous (such as his self-portrait during a dental examination). During the later 1970s he used infrared film to enliven familiar subjects, creating dramatic

5. **Sublimation of Blown Ice, Multnomah County, Oregon**, 1984
Selenium-toned gelatin silver print;
18 x 12 in.

effects to underscore his transformation of the actual subject to pictorial image. He was later drawn to landscapes and the movements contained in them: waves, changes in atmosphere, processes that suggest disorder and reorder.

Toedtemeier's camerawork and his geologic interests coalesced in the early 1980s, when he began to concentrate on the Columbia Gorge. Although he had experimented with a large-format camera in order to create images that would not show film grain and would record minute details, he soon switched to less cumbersome, medium-format cameras, which allowed him to navigate his chosen sites more easily. As he continued, he was able to re-create in his photographs a sense of being in the field, of traversing steep, rocky terrain, and of reaching rarely seen locations (see fig. 4). His earlier realization of the evidentiary—as well as metaphorical—nature of landforms manifested itself in a fascination for basalt—in his words, "the blood of the earth."[3] Its drama is a profound one: Toedtemeier's basalt subjects were formed from magmas coursing from deep within the earth, which blanketed much of northern and eastern Oregon between six and seventeen million years ago. He is drawn to details and specific features that express the character of individual formations (see fig. 1). Yet his direct, scientific approach to his subject matter is also charged with a sense of his awe, expressed through dramatic dualities of light and dark, of mass and void, of rough and smooth. These dualities, in turn, allude to the interlocking unities within Toedtemeier's vision, of idea and phenomenon, art and science, the hidden and the revealed, the temporal and the eternal. As he has written: "Thinking about the earth this way is part and parcel of thinking about our planetary system, ergo the cosmos / creation. Beauty runs through the whole of this in both visible and envisioned realities."[4]

1. Christopher Zinn, in *2001 Governor's Arts Awards* (Portland: Oregon Arts Commission, 2001), unpaginated.
2. Terry Toedtemeier to Sheryl Conkelton, 24 December 2001.
3. Quoted in Randy Gragg, "Time Frames," *Oregonian*, 24 September 1995.
4. Toedtemeier to Conkelton, 24 December 2001.

Patssi Valdez

*As an artist I hope to offer a glimpse of my own
personal vision of the world around me.*

2. **The Kitchen**, 1988
Acrylic on canvas; 48 x 36 in.
Collection of Curtis M. Hill, Los Angeles

1. **Black Virgin**, 1989
Acrylic on canvas; 36 x 24 in.
Collection of Diane Rodriguez and José
Delgado, Los Angeles

3. **Happy Birthday**, 2000
Acrylic on canvas; 44 x 72 in.
Collection of Cheech Marin

4. **Red Roses**, 1996
Acrylic on canvas; 30 x 24 in.
The Buck Collection, Laguna Beach, California

Patssi Valdez

NORIKO GAMBLIN

Patssi Valdez emerged as an artist in the early 1970s from

the discordant milieu of Los Angeles's barrio, where she grew up. She was one of ten thousand high school students from fifteen East Los Angeles public schools to participate in the landmark walkouts of 1968, in which classes were boycotted to protest an educational system that the students deemed shoddy and racist. On August 29, 1970, a few months after her high school graduation, she attended the Chicano Moratorium, the largest Latino demonstration against the Vietnam War, held in East Los Angeles. It was during this year that Valdez, who was attending East Los Angeles College while working at her mother's beauty shop, became part of an artists' collective that is considered today to have been a pioneer in combining performance art with social protest. Called Asco (Spanish for "nausea"), the group was composed of four members: Gronk, Valdez, and two of her former schoolmates, Harry Gamboa Jr. and Willie Herrón.

5. **A la Mode**, 1977
"No Movie" performance with Gronk, Patssi Valdez, and Harry Gamboa Jr.; gelatin silver print by Harry Gamboa Jr.

Through artworks and provocative public performances, Asco sought to heighten awareness of such issues as the negative stereotyping of Chicanos in the media, police harassment, a poor educational system, and various other forms of racism, both overt and insidious. Valdez played a central role in the group's innovative No Movies and Fotonovelas, photographic works that conflated elements of Mexican melodrama, Hollywood glamour, and barrio life. Often cast as a brazenly alluring and formidable heroine (see fig. 5), she confronted typical—and, to many, ideal—representations of demure and submissive Latinas. Her interrogation of feminine roles extended, at times, to the sphere of religion. On Christmas Eve in 1972, for example, Asco created its own parade for the community in response to the city's cancellation of the annual Christmas parade held on Whittier Boulevard. Valdez, dressed in a sparkling black gown and a "halo," played the Virgin of Guadalupe—a role that, as can be imagined, provoked considerable controversy.[1] Her self-presentation as the "dark Virgin" was groundbreaking, however, as Amalia Mesa-Bains has noted.[2]

Valdez left Asco in 1980 in order to attend art school—a lifelong dream—enrolling in Los Angeles's Otis Art Institute. Although it was not until 1988 (well after she had completed her M.F.A.) that she began painting, she soon developed a distinctive neo-expressionistic style, embracing the genre of the domestic interior. Her style fuses various aspects of early European modernism (particularly Vincent van Gogh's gestural brushstrokes, Henri Matisse's decorative patterning, and Cubism's deconstructed space) with elements drawn from Mexican and Chicano culture, including the vibrant color palette and the arrangements and types of things she depicts (religious objects in particular). Using a combination of skewed perspective, emphatic brushwork, and contrastive color harmonies, she creates tableaux situated within kitchens, bedrooms, dining rooms, and living rooms. Although generally uninhabited by human figures, these scenes are infused with a sense of human presence—in the form of portraits (hanging on walls or set on tables) or implied by still life–like arrangements, on dressers or family altars, of mementos and personal effects (see fig. 4).

For Valdez, the home not only signifies an arena traditionally associated with female identity—a long-standing concern within her art—but also serves as a personal metaphor for an interior state of mind. Thus, the world that she describes in her paintings, not surprisingly, is charged with energy emanating from diverse—and variously clashing—fields. At once captivating in their intense beauty of color, light, and form, and also perturbing in their strange, surrealistic irrationality (fruit bleeds, furniture rocks, and wine flies out of glasses), Valdez's paintings express a highly personal vision in which the familiar and mundane are transformed by the incendiary impulses of the imagination.

1. Tere Romo, "Patssi Valdez: A Precarious Comfort," in *Patssi Valdez: A Precarious Comfort/Una comodidad precaria* (San Francisco: Mexican Museum, 1999), 13. I am indebted to Romo's account of Valdez's early history and the history of Asco.
2. "[Valdez's] racialized Virgin images have a long trajectory, beginning in the mid-1970s with visionary feminist images that . . . can be seen as the first Chicana reconstructions of the Virgin of Guadalupe" (Amalia Mesa-Bains, "Spiritual Geographies," in *The Road to Aztlan: Art from a Mythic Homeland* [Los Angeles: Los Angeles County Museum of Art, 2001], 340).

Rick Bartow

Born 1946; resides in South Beach, Oregon
c/o Froelick Gallery, Portland, OR;
   (503) 222-1142

EDUCATION
B.A., Western Oregon State College, Monmouth, Oregon, 1969

SELECTED EXHIBITIONS
2002   *Rick Bartow: My Eye*, Hallie Ford Museum of Art,
          Willamette University, Salem, Oregon
2001   *Twelfth Street Series: Rick Bartow*, Tacoma Art Museum
2000   *Stories*, Schneider Museum of Art, Southern Oregon
          University, Ashland (solo)
1998   *Dance Harder!* Froelick Adelhart Gallery, Portland,
          Oregon (solo)
1997   *Rick Bartow: Drawings*, Yanagisawa Gallery, Saitama,
          Japan; Azabu Kasumicho, Tokyo
1996   Salamander Gallery, Arts Centre, Christchurch, New
          Zealand (solo)
1994   *The Oar of the Boat*, Peiper-Riegraf Gallery, Frankfurt (solo)
1993   *Truth Abandoned*, Gallery of Tribal Art, Vancouver,
          British Columbia (solo)
1992   *Wings and Sweat*, Jamison Thomas Gallery, Portland,
          Oregon (solo)
1988   Jamison Thomas Gallery, New York (solo)
1987   *R. E. Bartow: Recent Works*, American Indian
          Contemporary Art Gallery, San Francisco

SELECTED AWARDS AND HONORS
Brandywine Workshop Visiting Artist Fellowship, Philadelphia, 1988
Eiteljorg Fellowship for Native American Fine Art, Eiteljorg Museum of
   American Indians and Western Art, Indianapolis, 2001
Oregon Arts Commission, Fellowship in Visual Arts, 1987
Seattle Art Museum, Betty Bowen Special Recognition Award, 1990

SELECTED COLLECTIONS
Hallie Ford Museum of Art, Willamette University, Salem, Oregon
Heard Museum, Phoenix
Portland Art Museum, Portland, Oregon
Tacoma Art Museum
University of Oregon, Eugene
Westfalisches Landesmuseum, Münster

SELECTED BIBLIOGRAPHY
Caldwell, E. K. "Bartow: Conversation with an Artist." *Inkfish
   Magazine* 1 (June 1994): 3–5, 17.
Dobkins, Rebecca J. *Rick Bartow: My Eye*. Salem, Ore.: Hallie Ford
   Museum of Art, Willamette University, in association with
   University of Washington Press, 2002.
Dubin, Margaret. "Rick Bartow." *Indian Artist* 5 (winter 1999):
   36–41.
Marx, Doug. "Man behind the Mask." *Oregon Magazine*, March–April
   1988, 37–39.
Rushing, W. Jackson, III, ed. *After the Storm: The Eiteljorg
   Fellowship for Native American Fine Art*. Indianapolis: Eiteljorg
   Museum of American Indians and Western Art, 2001.
Smith, Tracy. "Rick Bartow at Froelick Adelhart." *Art in America* 85
   (July 1997): 100–101.
Wasserman, Abby. *R. E. Bartow*. Brochure. San Francisco: American
   Indian Contemporary Art Gallery, 1986.

Squeak Carnwath

Born 1947; resides in Oakland
Professor in residence, Department of Art
   Practice, University of California, Berkeley
c/o John Berggruen Gallery, San Francisco; www.berggruen.com

EDUCATION
M.F.A., California College of Arts and Crafts, Oakland, 1977
California College of Arts and Crafts, Oakland, 1970–71
Goddard College, Plainfield, Vermont, 1969–70

SELECTED EXHIBITIONS
2001   *Squeak Carnwath: Selected Paintings*, Fayerweather Gallery,
          University of Virginia, Charlottesville
          James Harris Gallery, Seattle (solo)
          Squeak Carnwath: Life Line, John Berggruen Gallery,
          San Francisco
2000   *Squeak Carnwath: Talking Pictures*, David Beitzel Gallery,
          New York
          Sweeney Art Gallery, University of California, Riverside (solo)
1999   *Squeak Carnwath: The Am-ness of Things*, Museum of
          Contemporary Art, Lake Worth, Florida
1998   *Squeak Carnwath: Seeing in the Dark*, Sonoma Museum of
          Visual Art, Santa Rosa, California
1995   *Squeak Carnwath: Eden in the Studio*, University Art
          Gallery, California State University, Stanislaus
1994   Chrysler Museum of Art, Norfolk, Virginia; San Jose Museum
          of Art, San Jose, California; Contemporary Museum,
          Honolulu (solo)
1992   *Squeak Carnwath: Recent Work*, Monterey Museum of Art,
          Monterey, California
1990   *Squeak Carnwath: Nature's Alchemy*, University Art Gallery,
          San Diego State University

SELECTED AWARDS AND HONORS
Alice Baber Art Award, 1990
John Simon Guggenheim Memorial Foundation, 1994
National Endowment for the Arts, 1980, 1985
San Francisco Museum of Modern Art, Society for the Encouragement
   of Contemporary Art, Award in Art, 1980
Yaddo, Saratoga Springs, New York, Alma B. C. Schapiro Residency
   for a Woman Painter, 1996

SELECTED COLLECTIONS
American Academy of Arts and Letters, New York
Berkeley Art Museum, University of California
Brooklyn Museum of Art
Oakland Museum of California
San Francisco Museum of Modern Art
Yale University Art Gallery, New Haven

SELECTED BIBLIOGRAPHY
Carnwath, Squeak. *Squeak Carnwath: Lists, Observations, and
   Counting*. San Francisco: Chronicle Books, 1996.
Cotter, Holland. "Art in Review: Squeak Carnwath at LedisFlam
   Gallery." *New York Times*, 17 September 1993, sec. C.
Frankel, David. "Squeak Carnwath at David Beitzel Gallery."
   Artforum 35 (October 1996): 116.
Goodman, Jonathan. "Squeak Carnwath at David Beitzel." *Art in
   America* 88 (December 2000): 125.
Smith, Roberta. "Squeak Carnwath at David Beitzel." *New York
   Times*, 31 May 1996, C22.

Linda Connor

Born 1944; resides in San Anselmo, California
Professor, Photography Department, San
   Francisco Art Institute
c/o 87 Rutherford, San Anselmo, CA 94960; (415) 459-3455

EDUCATION
M.S., Institute of Design, Illinois Institute of Technology, Chicago,
   1969
B.F.A., Rhode Island School of Design, Providence, 1967

SELECTED EXHIBITIONS
2001   *The Universe: A Convergence of Art, Music, and Science*,
      Armory Center for the Arts, Pasadena, California
      *Beyond Boundaries: Contemporary Photography in
      California*, Friends of Photography, Ansel Adams Center,
      San Francisco
      Recent Photographs: Linda Connor, Haines Gallery,
      San Francisco
      A Poem to Here: Photographs by Linda Connor, University of
      Wyoming Art Museum, Laramie
1999   *What Is Art For?* Oakland Museum of California
1996   *Linda Connor: Visits, Light Work*, Syracuse University,
      Syracuse, New York
      Stones of Faith, Stones of Peace, Jewish Museum San
      Francisco (solo)
1992   *Between Home and Heaven: Contemporary American
      Landscape Photography*, National Museum of American
      Art, Smithsonian Institution, Washington, D.C. (traveling)
      Earthly Constellations, San Francisco Museum of Modern
      Art; Museum of Photographic Arts, San Diego;
      Contemporary Museum, Honolulu; National Museum of
      American Art, Washington, D.C.; Joslyn Art Museum,
      Omaha (solo)
1990   *Spiral Journey*, Museum of Contemporary Photography,
      Columbia College, Chicago (solo)

SELECTED AWARDS AND HONORS
Charles Pratt Memorial Award, 1988
Friends of Photography, Photographer of the Year Award, 1986
John Simon Guggenheim Memorial Foundation, 1979
Marin Art Council, San Rafael, California, Lifetime Achievement
   Award, 1996
National Endowment for the Arts, 1976, 1988

SELECTED COLLECTIONS
Art Institute of Chicago
Museum of Modern Art, New York
San Francisco Museum of Modern Art
Smithsonian American Art Museum, Washington, D.C.
Yale University Art Gallery, New Haven

SELECTED BIBLIOGRAPHY
Connor, Linda. *Spiral Journey: Photographs, 1967–1990*. Chicago:
   Museum of Contemporary Photography, Columbia College, 1990.
———. *Luminance*. Carmel, Calif.: Center for Photographic Arts,
   1995.
———. *Visits: Linda Connor*. Syracuse, N.Y.: Light Work, 1996.
Connor, Linda, and Charles Simic. *On the Music of the Spheres*.
   New York: Library Fellows of the Whitney Museum of American
   Art, 1996.
Solos: Photographs by Linda Connor. Millerton, N.Y.: Apeiron
   Workshops, 1979.

Fernanda D'Agostino

Born 1950; resides in Portland, Oregon
c/o nandada@aol.com

EDUCATION
M.F.A., University of Montana, Missoula, 1984

SELECTED EXHIBITIONS AND PROJECTS
2001   *Theater of Memory/Secrets of Shadows*, Elizabeth Leach
      Gallery, Portland, Oregon (solo)
1996   *Imagining the Other Side*, Elizabeth Leach Gallery, Portland,
      Oregon (solo)
1995   *Wishing Trees*, Pioneer Courthouse Square, Portland, Oregon
      (solo)
1994   *Fate* (with Kristy Edmunds), Elizabeth Leach Gallery,
      Portland, Oregon
1993   *Abundance and Scarcity*, outdoor installation at Marylhurst
      College, Marylhurst, Oregon
1992   *Translations*, Elizabeth Leach Gallery, Portland, Oregon
      (solo)
1991   *Traveler's Rest* (collaboration with Dennis Kitsz), Randolph,
      Vermont
1989   *Offering*, The Art Gym, Marylhurst University
1986   *Third Western States Biennial*, Brooklyn Museum of Art
      In Bocca al Lupo (with Dennis Kitsz [sound]), Yellowstone
      Art Center, Billings, Montana
1985   Yellowstone Art Museum, Billings, Montana

SELECTED AWARDS AND HONORS
American Institute of Architects, Honor Award, 1999
On the Boards, Seattle, Artist's Project Grant, NEA Regional
   Initiatives Grant, 1994
Oregon Community Foundation, Bonnie Bronson Fellowship Award,
   1995
Regional Arts and Culture Council, Portland, Oregon, Project Grant,
   2000

SELECTED COLLECTIONS
Museum of Fine Arts, Houston
New York Public Library, Artist's Books Collection
Yellowstone Art Museum, Billings, Montana

SELECTED BIBLIOGRAPHY
Allan, Lois. *Contemporary Art in the Northwest*. Roseville East, New
   South Wales, Australia: Craftsman House, 1995.
Brenson, Michael. "How the Myths and Violence of the West Inspire
   Its Artists." *New York Times*, 15 June 1986.
Bruner, Cath. "Female Dominance in Public Art." *Arcade Magazine*
   18 (September 1999): 20–22.
Crandall, Gina. "Abundance and Scarcity." *Land Forum Magazine* 1,
   no. 3 (1999): 90–93.
McMorran, Megan. "A Death in the Family." *Oregonian*, 2 February
   1996.

James Doolin

1932–2002
c/o Koplin Gallery, Los Angeles; (310) 657-9843

EDUCATION
M.F.A., University of California, Los Angeles, 1971
New York University, 1960
Pratt Institute, Brooklyn, 1958–59
B.F.A., University of the Arts, Philadelphia, 1954

SELECTED EXHIBITIONS
2002   *James Doolin: Urban Invasion*, San Jose Museum of Art,
        San Jose, California
2000   *Representing L.A.*, Laguna Art Museum, Laguna Beach,
        California; South Texas Institute for the Arts, Corpus
        Christi; Frye Art Museum, Seattle
        Koplin Gallery, Los Angeles (solo; also 1984, 1986, 1992)
1992   *From the Studio: Recent Painting and Sculpture by Twenty
        California Artists*, Oakland Museum
1991   *California Cityscapes*, San Diego Museum of Art
1985   *Off the Street*, City of Los Angeles Cultural Affairs
        Department
1984   *Broad Spectrum: Contemporary Los Angeles Painters and
        Sculptors '84*, Design Center of Los Angeles
1978   *Shopping Mall: A Conceptual Perspective*, Victorian College
        of the Arts, Melbourne, Australia (solo, traveling)
1977   *Anatomy of a Painting*, Los Angeles Municipal Art Gallery
        (solo)
1968   *The Field*, National Gallery of Victoria, Melbourne, Australia;
        Art Gallery of New South Wales, Sydney (solo)

SELECTED AWARDS AND HONORS
Cultural Affairs Department, City of Los Angeles, C.O.L.A. Individual
    Artist Grant, 1997
John Simon Guggenheim Memorial Foundation, 1980
National Endowment for the Arts, 1981, 1985, 1991

SELECTED COLLECTIONS
National Gallery of Australia, Canberra
National Gallery of Victoria, Melbourne, Australia
Long Beach Museum of Art, Long Beach, California
Museum of Contemporary Art, Sydney
Yale University Art Gallery, New Haven

SELECTED BIBLIOGRAPHY
Auer, James. "Big City Squalor Provides a Focal Point for West Coast
    Artist Doolin." *Milwaukee Journal Sentinel*, 26 September 1993,
    sec. E.
Clothier, Peter. "James Doolin." *Art in America* 72 (September
    1984): 220, 223.
Forgács, Éva. "James Doolin." *Art Issues* 62 (March–April 2000): 41.
Gilbert, Rick. "James Doolin at Grand Central Art Center Gallery."
    Artweek 30 (May 1999): 24–25.
Knight, Christopher. "Capturing the Transience of 'Some Los Angeles
    Icons.'" *Los Angeles Times*, 21 January 2000, Calendar sec.
Wilson, William. "Two Painters Who Clarify." *Los Angeles Times*, 27
    March 1977, Calendar sec.

Gaylen Hansen

Born 1921; resides in Palouse, Washington
Professor Emeritus, Fine Arts Department,
    Washington State University, Pullman
c/o Linda Hodges Gallery, Seattle; lhodges@lindahodgesgallery.com

EDUCATION
M.F.A., University of Southern California, Los Angeles, 1953
B.F.A., Utah State Agricultural College, Logan, 1953
Otis Art Institute, Los Angeles, 1939–40

SELECTED EXHIBITIONS
1999   Linda Hodges Gallery, Seattle (solo)
1996   Redmann Galerie, Berlin (solo)
1994   Koplin Gallery, Los Angeles (solo)
1991   Redmann Galerie, Berlin (solo)
1990   Arts Club of Chicago (solo)
1988   Yellowstone Art Center, Billings, Montana (solo)
1985   *Gaylen Hansen: Paintings of a Decade, 1975–1985*,
        Museum of Art, Washington State University, Pullman;
        Seattle Art Museum; San Jose Museum of Art, San Jose,
        California; Los Angeles Municipal Art Gallery
1983   Monique Knowlton Gallery, New York (solo; also 1980,
        1981)
1981   Glenbow Museum, Calgary, Canada (solo)
1959   Seattle Art Museum (solo)

SELECTED AWARDS AND HONORS
New Museum, New York, Sambuca Romana Prize, 1984
Washington State, Governor's Arts Award, 1989

SELECTED COLLECTIONS
Chase Manhattan Bank
Encompass Europe, Munich
Honolulu Academy of Arts
Microsoft Art Collection, Redmond, Washington
Seattle Art Museum
Tacoma Art Museum

SELECTED BIBLIOGRAPHY
Guenther, Bruce. "The Eccentric and Personal Vision of Gaylen
    Hansen." In *Gaylen Hansen: Paintings of a Decade, 1975–1985*.
    Pullman: Washington State University Press; Museum of Art,
    Washington State University, 1985.
Hackett, Regina. "In His Old Age, a Painter Finds Rage, Elegance,
    and a Fiery Wit." *Seattle Post-Intelligencer*, 14 April 1995.
Halper, Vicki. "Gaylen Hansen." In *Gaylen Hansen*. Seattle: Linda
    Hodges Gallery in association with University of Washington Press,
    2001.
Hammond, Pamela. *Gaylen Hansen*. Chicago: Arts Club of Chicago,
    1990.
Philipps, Deborah C. "Gaylen Hansen." *Art News* 81 (January 1982):
    162, 164.
White, Peter. *Gaylen Hansen*. Calgary, Canada: Glenbow Museum,
    1981.

Mary Henry

Born 1913; resides in Freeland, Washington
c/o Bryan Ohno Gallery, Seattle;
  www.bryanohnogallery.com

EDUCATION
M.A., Institute of Design, Chicago, 1946
B.F.A., California College of Arts and Crafts, Oakland, 1938

SELECTED EXHIBITIONS
2001   *Mary Henry: No Limits*, Bellevue Art Museum, Bellevue,
          Washington
          Modern Master Works, Bryan Ohno Gallery, Seattle
          In the Gardens of Myth and Logic, Museum of Northwest
          Art, La Conner, Washington (two-person show)
2000   *Bumberbiennale: Painting 2000*, Bumbershoot, Seattle
          American Abstract Artists Group, Hillwood Art Museum,
          Long Island University, Brookville, New York
          Mary Henry: Paintings from 1968 and 1998, PDX Gallery,
          Portland, Oregon
1997   *The Geometric Tradition in American Art*, Meyerson/
          Nowinski Art Associates, Seattle
1995   *Mary Henry: Selected Paintings*, Linda Cannon Gallery,
          Seattle
1992   Tacoma Art Museum (solo)
1988   *Mary Henry: Selected Works*, Whatcom Museum of History
          and Art, Bellingham, Washington
1985   Open Space Gallery, Victoria, British Columbia (solo)
1969   Arleigh Gallery, San Francisco (solo)

SELECTED AWARDS AND HONORS
Corporate Council for the Arts, Seattle, Annual Poster Award, 1996
King County Public Art Program, Washington, Honors Program, 2001

SELECTED COLLECTIONS
Institute of Design, Illinois Institute of Technology
Portland Art Museum, Oregon
Safeco, Seattle
Seattle Art Museum
Seattle Arts Commission
Tacoma Art Museum

SELECTED BIBLIOGRAPHY
Brunsman, Laura, and Ruth Askey. *Modernism and Beyond: Women
    Artists of the Pacific Northwest*. New York: Midmarch Arts, 1993.
French, Palmer D. "San Francisco: Mary Henry at Arleigh Gallery."
    Artforum 8 (October 1969): 75–76.
Kangas, Matthew. "Mary Henry: American Constructivist." *Women's
    Art Journal* 12 (fall 1991–winter 1992): 20.
Lindberg, Ted. "Living for Geometry." *Reflex* 9 (December–January
    1996): 12.
West, Harvey. *The Washington Years: A Contemporary View, 1980–
    1981*. Seattle: Henry Art Gallery, University of Washington, 1982.

Mildred Howard

Born 1945; resides in Berkeley, California
c/o Gallery Paule Anglim, San Francisco;
  www.gallerypauleanglim.com

EDUCATION
M.F.A., John F. Kennedy University, 1985
A.A., College of Alameda, 1977

SELECTED EXHIBITIONS
2001   Gallery Paule Anglim, San Francisco (solo)
1999   *In the Line of Fire*, Gallery II, University of Bradford,
          England; City Gallery, Leicester, England (solo)
1998   *S. S. (Slave Stealer)*, Institute of Contemporary Art, Boston
          (solo)
1997   *Crossings*, Berkeley Art Center, Berkeley, California (solo)
1995   *Seeing the Soul*, Oakland Museum of California
1994   Nielsen Gallery, Boston (solo)
1992   *Art in the Anchorage*, Creative Time, New York
          Tap: Investigation of Memory, INTAR Gallery, New York
          (solo)
1991   *Ten Little Children Standing in a Line (One Got Shot and
          Then There Were Nine)*, Adaline Kent Award Exhibition,
          Walter McBean Gallery, San Francisco Art Institute (solo)
1989   *Tap: Investigation of Memory*, Walter McBean Gallery, San
          Francisco Art Institute (solo)
1984   *Gospel and the Storefront Church*, InterArts of Marin,
          California, installation in the Old Post Office, Mill Valley,
          California (solo)

SELECTED AWARDS AND HONORS
Anonymous Was a Woman Awards, 2000
Bank of America Award, Oakland, 1975
Fleishhacker Foundation, Eureka Fellowship, 1996
Lila Wallace–Reader's Digest Foundation, 1992
National Endowment for the Arts, 1992
Rockefeller Foundation, Bellagio Study and Conference Center,
    Bellagio, Italy, 1996

SELECTED COLLECTIONS
Oakland Museum of California
San Francisco International Airport
San Jose Museum of Art, San Jose, California
Wadsworth Atheneum, Hartford
Washington State Arts Commission

SELECTED BIBLIOGRAPHY
Barron, Stephanie, et al. *Made in California: Art, Image, and
    Identity, 1900–2000*. Los Angeles: Los Angeles County Museum
    of Art, 2000.
Janson, H. W., *History of Art*. 5th edition. Revised and expanded by
    Anthony F. Janson. New York: Harry N. Abrams, 1995.
Lacy, Suzanne, ed. *Mapping the Terrain: New Genre Public Art*.
    Seattle: Bay Press, 1995.
LeFalle-Collins, Lizzetta. *Emerging Artists, New Expressions, 1990*.
    Los Angeles: California Afro-American Museum Foundation, 1990.
Lewis, Samella, ed. *Art: African American*. Los Angeles: Handcraft
    Studios, 1990.
Schacter, Daniel L. *Searching for Memory: The Brain, the Mind, and
    the Past*. New York: Basic Books, 1996.

Mary Lee Hu

Born 1943; resides in Seattle, Washington
Professor, Metals Program, School of Art,
  University of Washington
c/o mhu@u.washington.edu

EDUCATION
M.F.A., Southern Illinois University, Carbondale, 1967
B.F.A., Cranbrook Academy of Art, Bloomfield Hills, Michigan, 1965
Miami University, Oxford, Ohio, 1961–63

SELECTED EXHIBITIONS
2000   *Curves Revisited*, Susan Cummins Gallery, Mill Valley,
         California (solo)
1994   *Mary Lee Hu: Master Metalsmith*, National Ornamental
         Metal Museum, Memphis
1993   *Sculptural Concerns: Contemporary American
         Metalworking*, Contemporary Arts Center, Cincinnati;
         Fort Wayne Museum of Art (traveling)
1989   *Mary Lee Hu: Goldsmith*, Merrin Gallery, New York
1987   *The Eloquent Object*, Philbrook Museum of Art, Tulsa
         (traveling)
1986   *Craft Today: Poetry of the Physical*, American Craft
         Museum, New York (traveling)
1980   *International Jewelry, 1900-1980*, World Crafts Council
         Conference, Künstlerhaus, Vienna
1978   *Silver in American Life*, Yale University Art Museum, New
         Haven, Connecticut (traveling)
1974   *Goldsmith/74*, Renwick Gallery, National Museum of
         American Art, Smithsonian Institution, Washington,
         D.C.; Minnesota Museum of American Art, Saint Paul
         (traveling)
1969   *Young Americans '69*, Museum of Contemporary Crafts,
         New York (traveling)

SELECTED AWARDS AND HONORS
American Craft Council, 1996
National Endowment for the Arts, 1976, 1984, 1992
Smithsonian American Art Museum, Washington, D.C., James
  Renwick Alliance of the Renwick Gallery, Master of the Medium,
  1999

SELECTED COLLECTIONS
American Craft Museum, New York
Art Institute of Chicago
Museum of Fine Arts, Boston
Renwick Gallery, Smithsonian American Art Museum,
  Washington, D.C.
Victoria and Albert Museum, London

SELECTED BIBLIOGRAPHY
Benesh, Carolyn. "Mary Lee Hu." *Ornament Magazine* 6 (spring
  1983): 2–5, 11.
Breckenridge, Elizabeth. "Mary Lee Hu: High on the Wire." *Craft
  Horizons* 37 (April 1977): 40–43, 65.
DuPriest, Karen. "Craft into Art: Mary Lee Hu Takes Gold and Silver
  Jewelry in a New Direction." *Connoisseur Magazine* 216 (October
  1986): 137–41.
"Goldsmithing: Mary Lee Hu." Directed by Peggy Case. *Art Minutes*.
  KCTS Public Broadcasting Television, Seattle, 6 September 1993.
Mahler, Annette. "Mary Lee Hu: The Purpose and Persistence of
  Wire." *Metalsmith* 9 (winter 1989): 24–29.

Adrian Saxe

Born 1943; resides in Los Angeles
Professor, Department of Art, University of
  California, Los Angeles
c/o 4835 North Figueroa Street, Los Angeles, CA 90024

EDUCATION
B.F.A., California Institute of the Arts, 1974

SELECTED EXHIBITIONS
2001   *USA Clay*, Renwick Gallery, Smithsonian American Art
         Museum, Washington, D.C.
2000   *Color and Fire: Defining Moments in Studio Ceramics,
         1950–2000*, Los Angeles County Museum of Art
         (traveling)
         Garth Clark Gallery, New York (solo)
         Departures: Eleven Artists at the Getty, J. Paul Getty
         Museum, Los Angeles
1999   *Artisti dal mondo*, invitational component of
         *Manifestazioni internazionali della ceramica d'arte
         contemporanea—51° Premio Faenza*, Museo
         Internazionale della Ceramiche di Faenza, Italy
         Art and Industry: Contemporary Porcelain from Sèvres,
         American Craft Museum, New York
         *The Art of Craft: Contemporary Works from the Saxe
         Collection*, M. H. De Young Memorial Museum, San
         Francisco
1998   *Clay into Art: Selections from the Contemporary
         Ceramics Collection in the Metropolitan Museum of
         Art*, Metropolitan Museum of Art, New York
1995   *The White House Collection of American Crafts*,
         National Museum of American Art, Smithsonian
         Institution, Washington, D.C. (traveling)
1993   *The Clay Art of Adrian Saxe*, Los Angeles County
         Museum of Art; Museum of Contemporary Ceramic Art,
         Shigaraki, Japan; Newark Museum, New Jersey

SELECTED AWARDS AND HONORS
American Craft Council, 2000
Association dialog entre les cultures and United States Information
  Agency, U.S./France Exchange Fellowship, 1987
Atelier experimental de recherche et de création de la Manufacture
  nationale de Sèvres, residency fellowship, 1983–84, 1987
National Endowment for the Arts, 1986

SELECTED COLLECTIONS
Cooper-Hewitt, National Design Museum, Smithsonian Institution
Everson Museum of Art, Syracuse, New York
Kunstuitleen Museum Het Kruithuis, The Netherlands
Los Angeles County Museum of Art
Metropolitan Museum of Art, New York
Musée du Louvre, Paris
Oakland Museum of California
Victoria and Albert Museum, London

SELECTED BIBLIOGRAPHY
Corrin, Lisa G., and Joaneath Spicer, eds. *Going for Baroque:
  Eighteen Contemporary Artists Fascinated with the Baroque and
  Rococo*. Baltimore: Contemporary Museum; Walters Art Gallery,
  1995.
Lynn, Martha Drexler. *The Clay Art of Adrian Saxe*. New York:
  Thames and Hudson, 1993.

Terry Toedtemeier

Born 1947; resides in Portland, Oregon
c/o PDX Contemporary Art, Portland, OR;
 www.pdxcontemporaryart.com

EDUCATION

B.S., Oregon State University, Corvallis, 1969

SELECTED EXHIBITIONS

2001 *Between Light and Shadow: Photographs and Prints from the Gary Bettis Collection*, Boise Art Museum, Boise, Idaho

2000 *Invasive Basalt*, PDX Gallery, Portland, Oregon (solo)

1998 *The Collection of Richard and Judith Smooke*, Sun Valley Center for the Arts, Sun Valley, Idaho

1997 *Terry Toedtemeier: Photographs*, Museum of Fine Arts, University of Montana, Missoula

1995 *Basalt Exposures*, The Art Gym, Marylhurst College, Marylhurst, Oregon (solo)

1992 *Between Home and Heaven: Contemporary American Landscape Photography*, National Museum of American Art, Smithsonian Institution, Washington, D.C. (traveling)

1988 *Road and Roadside: American Photographs, 1930–1986*, Art Institute of Chicago; San Francisco Museum of Modern Art

1987 *America's Uncommon Places: The Blessings of Liberty*, Sumner School Museum and Archives, National Trust for Historic Preservation

1986 *Terry Toedtemeier: Photographs*, Vollum College Center, Reed College, Portland, Oregon

1979 *The Collection of Joseph and Elaine Monson*, Henry Art Gallery, University of Washington, Seattle

SELECTED AWARDS AND HONORS

Joshua Tree National Park, Artist in Residence, 2001
National Endowment for the Arts, 1979
Oregon Arts Commission, Masters Fellowship, 1990
Regional Arts and Culture Council, Portland, Oregon, Visual Artist Fellowship, 2000

SELECTED COLLECTIONS

Art Museum, Princeton University
Portland Art Museum, Portland, Oregon
San Francisco Museum of Modern Art
Seattle Art Museum
Smithsonian American Art Museum, Washington, D.C.

SELECTED BIBLIOGRAPHY

Allan, Lois. *Contemporary Art in the Northwest*. Roseville East, New South Wales, Australia: Craftsman House, 1995.

Foresta, Merry A., Stephen Jay Gould, and Karal Ann Marling. *Between Home and Heaven: Contemporary American Landscape Photography from the Consolidated Natural Gas Company Collection of the National Museum of American Art*, Smithsonian Institution. Washington, D.C.: National Museum of American Art, Smithsonian Institution, 1992.

Smith, Tracy. "Terry Toedtemeier at the Art Gym." *Art in America* 84 (April 1996): 123–24.

Taylor, Sue. "Terry Toedtemeier at PDX." *Art in America* 89 (April 2001): 149–50.

Toedtemeier, Terry. *Basalt Exposures*. Marylhurst, Ore.: Art Gym, Marylhurst College, 1995.

Patssi Valdez

Born 1951; resides in Los Angeles
c/o Patricia Correia Gallery, Los Angeles;
 www.correiagallery.com

EDUCATION

B.F.A., Otis Art Institute, Los Angeles, 1985
Parsons School of Design, New York, 1980–84

SELECTED EXHIBITIONS

2001 *Arte Latino: Treasures from the Smithsonian American Art Museum*, Smithsonian American Art Museum, Washington, D.C.

2000 *Made in California: Art, Image, and Identity, 1900–2000*, Los Angeles County Museum of Art

 Twelve Divas, Molly Barnes Gallery, Santa Monica, California

 Patricia Correia Gallery, Santa Monica, California (solo)

1999 *A Precarious Comfort*, Mexican Museum, San Francisco; Laguna Art Museum, Laguna Beach, California (solo)

1998 *Patssi Valdez: Private Landscapes, 1988–1998*, Art Galleries, California State University, Northridge

1996 *Mythic Present of Chagoya, Valdez, and Gronk*, Fisher Gallery, University of Southern California, Los Angeles

 Maiden America, Laguna Art Museum, Laguna Beach, California

 Ceremony of Spirit: Nature and Memory in Contemporary Latino Art, Mexican Museum, San Francisco; Laguna Art Museum, Laguna Beach, California; Boise Art Museum, Idaho; Fresno Art Museum, Fresno, California; Studio Museum in Harlem, New York

1995 *Patssi Valdez: A Room of One's Own*, San Jose Museum of Art, San Jose, California

SELECTED AWARDS AND HONORS

Brody Arts Fund, 1998
Durfee Foundation, 1999
J. Paul Getty Trust Fund for the Visual Arts, California Community Foundation, 1998
National Endowment for the Arts, 1989, 1994

SELECTED COLLECTIONS

Laguna Art Museum, Laguna Beach, California
Mexican Fine Arts Center Museum, Chicago
Mexican Museum, San Francisco
Smithsonian American Art Museum, Washington, D.C.
Tucson Museum of Art, Tucson, Arizona

SELECTED BIBLIOGRAPHY

Merrero, Letisha. "Latinas of the Year, 1999." *Latina Magazine* 4 (September 1999): 72.

Muñoz, Lorenza. "A Painter's Great Escape." *Los Angeles Times*, 7 March 1999, Calendar sec.

Nieto, Margarita. "Patssi Valdez." *Latin American Art* 2 (summer 1991): 57.

Torres, Anthony. "Patssi Valdez at the San Jose Museum of Art." *Artweek* 26 (9 December 1995): 20–21.

Welles, Elenore. "Patssi Valdez." *Artscene* 20 (December 2000): 14–15.

Wilson, William. "Precious Child Shows an Artist Maturing." *Los Angeles Times*, 21 February 1998, Calendar sec.

Acknowledgments

The Awards for Visual Artists depend on an ever-broadening circle of friends to take shape. We are pleased to convene a growing community of artists and arts professionals under the aegis of the 2001–2002 Flintridge program.

The Flintridge Foundation is most grateful to the people with the most difficult task: the panelists who selected the recipients. The two juries (for California and for Oregon and Washington) had to interpret new guidelines and choose twelve artists total from a daunting number of applicants. In this cycle we had the pleasure of working with LaMar Harrington, director emeritus, Bellevue Art Museum; Terri M. Hopkins, director/curator, The Art Gym, Marylhurst University; and Beth Sellars, curator/collection manager, Public and Community Arts, Seattle Arts Commission, and curator, Suyama Space, on the Oregon and Washington awards. We were fortunate to have an equally outstanding group of panelists for the California awards: Ellen Fleurov, formerly museum director, California Center for the Arts, Escondido; Philip E. Linhares, chief curator, Oakland Museum of California Art; and Larry Thomas, artist and vice president and dean of academic affairs, San Francisco Art Institute. We thank the panelists for their efforts on behalf of artists, their community, and the foundation.

While panel members rotate each cycle, the foundation's Artists Advisory Group has provided constancy and sage counsel since 1996. In this cycle we depended on Ann Chamberlain, James Lavadour, and Norie Sato to express the voices of artists and help us develop new language to describe our selection criteria, conduct successful application workshops in Oregon and Washington, and find wise and generous panelists. We are sad to announce that James Lavadour is rotating off the Advisory Group, but we thank him for his many contributions. Flintridge is pleased to welcome Larry Thomas as a new adviser.

Another constant in our circle of friends has been the publication team. Now that the awards honor artists who have yet to achieve national renown, the catalogue plays a more important role in increasing the visibility and recognition of the Flintridge recipients. To accomplish this goal, we are pleased to count on longtime colleagues editor and writer Noriko Gamblin, editor Karen Jacobson, writer Sheryl Conkelton, and designer Susan Silton, who—with the assistance of our director of programs, Pam Wolkoff, and our program officer, Angie Kim—have produced a publication of uncompromising quality. We also thank the awards recipients for their patience and their participation in developing the catalogue.

The Flintridge Foundation is guided by the wisdom of its board of directors, and we thank its members for believing in the awards program. Because they value artists and creativity, because they continually strive for improvement, and because they trust the awards process, the board members make this program possible, and we are grateful. We recognize the awards program staff members—Pam Wolkoff, Angie Kim, Karen Gerst, and Yvonne Taylor—for their attention to the program's goals and values. Pam Wolkoff has provided critical guidance that has shaped the awards program, and we thank her for her thoughtful leadership and her sustained commitment to the program and the artists it recognizes. Angie Kim deserves special recognition for organizing and conducting the program's first outreach workshops in 2001, and we thank our partner organizations, Seattle's Artist Trust and Portland's Regional Arts and Culture Council, for their assistance in reaching out to more artists.

Finally, we recognize all of the remarkable artists we serve: the current awards recipients and the other applicants who have been exploring their ideas and building artistic practices for more than twenty years. They humble us. We are awed by their commitment to their craft and to their vision, and the Flintridge Foundation appreciates the opportunity to serve this magnificent community of artists.

Jaylene Moseley
Managing Director
Flintridge Foundation

Awards History

1999/2000

Awards Recipients
Lia Cook
Harry Gamboa Jr.
Douglas Hall
Paul Kos
Suzanne Lacy
Daniel Joseph Martinez
Michael C. McMillen
Lari Pittman
Alison Saar
Peter Shelton
Buster Simpson
Larry Sultan

Panelists
Anne Ayres
Armando Rascón
Christopher Rauschenberg
Jake Seniuk
Gail Tremblay

1997/1998

Awards Recipients
Chris Burden
John Divola
Lynn Hershman
David Ireland
Tom Marioni
Ron Nagle
Noah Purifoy
Nancy Rubins
Betye Saar
Mark Thompson
Carlos Villa
Al Wong

Panelists
Vicki Harper
Margaret Honda
George Longfish
Mia McEldowney
Catherine Wagner

Artists Advisory Group
Ann Chamberlain
James Lavadour
Norie Sato

John Outterbridge (1996–98)
Joe Soldate (1996–98)

Flintridge Foundation

Board of Directors

Armando Gonzalez
President

Alexander Moseley
Vice President

Susan Addison
Secretary

Gordon Hamilton
Treasurer

Mona Heinze

Judith Johnson

Ann Moseley Morris

Cassandra Moseley

David Moseley

Program Staff

Jaylene Moseley
Managing Director

Pam Wolkoff
*Director of Programs,
Arts and Conservation*

Angie Kim
Program Officer, Arts

Karen Gerst
Communications Officer

Yvonne Taylor
*Program Assistant and
Events Coordinator, Arts*